Studying English Literature

Marian Cox

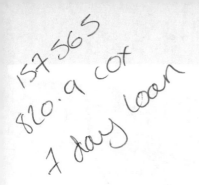

LRC Stoke Park
GUILDFORD COLLEGE

Philip Allan Updates
Market Place
Deddington
Oxfordshire
OX15 0SE

Orders
Bookpoint Ltd, 130 Milton Park, Abingdon, Oxfordshire, OX14 4SB
tel: 01235 827720
fax: 01235 400454
e-mail: uk.orders@bookpoint.co.uk
Lines are open 9.00 a.m.–5.00 p.m., Monday to Saturday, with a 24-hour message
answering service. You can also order through the Philip Allan Updates website:
www.philipallan.co.uk

© Philip Allan Updates 2005

ISBN 978-1-84489-400-0

Printed in Malta

Philip Allan Updates' policy is to use papers that are natural, renewable and
recyclable products and made from wood grown in sustainable forests. The logging
and manufacturing processes are expected to conform to the environmental regu-
lations of the country of origin.

P01013

Studying English Literature

Contents

Introduction

Aims of the guide

The purpose of this Student Guide to *Studying English Literature at Advanced Level* is to deepen your understanding of how literature works, to enable you to respond appropriately to literary texts and to address the particular requirements of examination Assessment Objectives (AOs). It is assumed that you have read a variety of genres of literary text at Key Stage 3 (KS3) and have studied set texts at GCSE, and that you are therefore familiar with the basic terminology of and approaches to literary texts. It is intended that this Student Guide will provide an initial general background to A-level study and an introduction to the skills to be developed and assessed. It can be read as a whole or dipped into in any order and used as a reference guide to specific aspects of the A-level course. It provides a number of summaries, lists, analyses, guides and resources as support for literary studies. The overall aim of the guide is to encourage the development of your personal response as an informed reader of literary texts.

The *Theory and background* section gives general information about contextual and theoretical aspects of literary studies and raises issues relevant to the A-level course. *Approaches to literary texts* helps you to find a way into set texts that is tailored to their genre and reminds you of the skills required and the aspects to be considered when preparing a set text. *Assessment focus* gives detailed support for the revision and practice period leading up to the exam and advice on exam technique. *Resources* provides historical and critical overviews and a comprehensive glossary of literary terminology.

What makes a successful English Literature student?

Maturity is an important factor and used to be the argument given for A-level Literature remaining a linear rather than becoming a modular exam. If you are embarrassed by sex, shocked by homosexuality, intolerant of other races, have fundamental religious beliefs or hold extreme political views, then this probably isn't the subject for you. Open-mindedness — which is not the same as having no opinions — is a prerequisite for the good literature student. The works you will be studying were written for adults and assume a familiarity with the ways of the world, particularly regarding relationships. Personal experience is the interface between text and reader.

Without an interest in language and the way it works, it is difficult to be a successful literature student. Although GCSE studies may unfortunately have given you the idea that language and literature are two different subjects, it isn't true. Literature is constructed from language, and without a recognition of the types of brick and methods of joinery being used, you cannot appreciate the building. Committed literature students read in every spare moment — in the bath, in bed, on the bus — and build up a 'reading ego'. They become independent and critical readers, not just voracious ones. They read for underlying patterns and for overview, not just for character and plot — the superficial elements of text — and develop sensitivity to recurring imagery within and between texts.

If you were reading an essay about a work of literature, would you be convinced by the argument being presented if it were full of inaccuracies of language use, as in poor spelling, ungrammatical expression or inadequate punctuation? Your analysis and evaluation of a writer's language are inevitably suspect if you reveal an inability to use it accurately yourself. Furthermore, without a degree of competence in your own expression, you cannot convey your observations clearly to others. The cultivation of essay techniques and style are skills that require regular practice and it is especially necessary to write literature essays frequently if your other A-level subjects do not require essay writing.

Wider reading

According to Fay Weldon, 'If you read a lot, the world of exams is an easy nut to crack.' Not being a reader sets up a vicious circle of reluctance: the desire to read comes from enjoyment, which comes from confidence, which comes from understanding, which comes from competence, which comes from practice. Through regular private reading you become better able to compare, interpret and evaluate texts; through expressing your insights to others you learn to support opinions and take into account those of other readers. Wider reading helps you to appreciate social and historical context to be able to put your set authors into perspective and in their different genres and periods. These are essential A-level skills, and exam boards expect you to read more during your literature course than just the four or eight set texts.

How do you normally choose a fiction book to read, when browsing in a bookshop, library or along a friend's bookshelf? The following five-stage process is a safe way of checking whether a book would suit your taste and interests, and will usually safeguard you from wasting your time and money on something you will find yourself unable to read to the end. You can reject books at different stages of the process if they do not appeal to you. As you get more experienced at selecting your reading and more knowledgeable about authors and publishers, you will be able to skip straight to stage 4.

(1) Look at the cover design, which will give you a clue to the likely genre and content. Be aware, however, that some covers are deliberately misleading, particularly if they have been produced especially for a film tie-in.

(2) Let your mind dwell on the title for a moment. What does it suggest? Do any associations come to mind? If you enjoyed the film at all, read the book as well, since all film adaptations remove material from the original book, sometimes disastrously.

(3) Notice the author's name. What do you know or what have you heard about this writer? Has the author been short-listed for prizes? Have you read anything else by this writer? Did you like or hate it or can't you remember? Generally speaking, the author is a better guarantee of suitability to your taste than the title. Bear in mind that some writers use initials to conceal their gender, some use different names for different genres and some write both adult and children's fiction.

(4) Turn over and read the blurb on the back cover. Does it sound like your kind of book? How much of a cliché does the plot appear to be? When and where is the narrative set?

(5) Read the first paragraph or half page of the novel. Are you interested? Do you feel like reading on? If you do, the chances are that you have chosen the right book.

Your teachers should be able to provide you with a list of appropriate wider reading for A-level students. No recommended reading list can be exhaustive or definitive, and no student would find all of the recommendations to his or her taste. Lists also need to be updated continually as new works are published. A useful compilation will include the best-known and generally acclaimed works of prose fiction, drama and poetry: those that crop up regularly on other lists, have won major prizes, stay in print and that many educated people have at least heard of. It should also cover a range of historical and cultural backgrounds, fiction genres and levels of accessibility, so that there is plenty of choice for everyone. From time to time, magazines publish lists of the most popular fiction texts of all time, which at least give an indication of those that may offer enjoyment and value.

Positive attitude

Interim grades are not a judgement upon you as a person, or even an indication of what you will get in one or two years' time; they are to help you to move onwards and upwards. Students and teachers often observe that the jump from GCSE to AS English Literature is considerable, and you may well feel not only that the subject has changed, but also that your grades are not what you were used to getting at GCSE. But why should they be? If you could get a grade A within the first few weeks of starting A-level work, you would not need to follow the course at all. After GCSE you have to adapt to a higher level, as you do in any other subject, although of course you already have the basic skills to be developed. Expect to get grade Cs and even grade Ds for your first essays, if they are being marked to standard, and consider that to be a good start. Do not necessarily expect different A-level teachers to give you the same grades; perhaps you feel more engaged by one text or teaching style than by another. What matters is that you learn from each experience and show improvement the next time, so that with normal progression you can then reasonably hope for As and Bs by the end of the first year (before the next jump to A2).

Students who make good progress pay more attention to the accompanying comments than to the grade itself. However, you should ask for further explanation if you do not understand a mark or if it does not appear to reflect the assessment criteria. So instead of resenting low marks — or becoming complacent about high ones — use your teachers as resources for knowledge and support. Be prepared to take responsibility for your own learning, rather than looking for someone to blame for any lack of progress.

The learning process lies in the application of advice. If you avoid writing essays for any reason, you cannot hope to improve and no one can help you to do so. A poor essay is always better than no essay, as at least it has given you practice and now both you and your teacher know what your problems are and how you can tackle them next time. You may well feel under pressure, especially if your other AS or A2 subjects are heavy on reading and writing (history and English is a common but demanding combination) and it is easy to get into the bad habit of making your other subjects the excuse for not doing your English essay, and vice versa. Good students know the necessity of constant practice in all their subjects and find time to fit them all in through organisation and prioritisation.

Teachers at A-level have their own personal enthusiasms and specialities, and you will inevitably notice differences of approach, but do not judge one to be better than the other or try to play them off against each other. If you have more than one teacher, they will provide a variety of insights and interpretations, and what does not suit you may appeal to others in the class. Criticism and advice are meant to be constructive and supportive, not a provocation or excuse to switch off, and more demanding teachers may be more conducive to success for their students than easy-going ones, so don't allow personalities to become a problem.

Regardless of whether or not you enjoyed your KS3 or KS4 Shakespeare texts or your other GCSE set books, this is a fresh start and you shouldn't allow previous experiences to prejudice you. Not only are these new texts and new approaches — and probably new teachers — but you too will have changed. You may now be ready for authors or genres you did not appreciate when you were younger, and you will continue to develop as a reader throughout the course. Judging by surveys, you are likely, for instance, to value and enjoy poetry more by the end of the course than at the beginning. It may seem strange that you will be studying only four books per year, but this does not mean that you can be leisurely in your work habits; enlightenment, expertise and reaching examination standard come from thorough study and extensive rereading.

Taking against a text, and convincing yourself you are going to do badly on it, is another recipe for underachievement. You may already have views on what you like and don't like, but how can you widen your knowledge and enjoyment if you are not willing to give other genres and periods a chance? At the start of the course most students are more familiar with novels than with poetry, and with contemporary rather than earlier works, which makes them think that they will prefer the study of modern prose. You don't have this exclusive option, so you might as well approach all texts with equal receptiveness.

Obstacles to success

Teachers have responsibilities towards students, and various practices and situations can adversely affect the performance of the class as a whole: lack of knowledge and preparation; overgenerous marking; excessive criticism; setting insufficient homework; lack of useful monitoring and feedback; uninspiring or confusing lessons; pace too slow or fast; level too easy or too difficult; unsuitable text choices. Factors beyond the teacher's control may also affect teaching and learning methodologies and outcomes, such as the class being too large or too small; widely differing ability levels within the group; shortage of timetabled lessons; overfragmentation of course between teachers; frequent teacher absence; lack of experience or confidence of teacher.

However, the main barriers to students achieving maximum performance at A-level, regardless of their potential ability or previous achievement, are those over which students have some control. The list below covers the attitudes, habits and situations that reduce the likelihood of success:

- irregular and infrequent attendance at lessons
- poor punctuality
- lack of commitment to subject
- not taking notes in class
- taking dictation in class
- unwillingness to admit to not understanding something or to needing help
- avoidance of homework and essay writing
- distraction of other interests or demands on time
- poor organisation and time management
- forgetting to bring text to class
- coming unprepared to class
- reluctance to work independently
- 'coasting' because other students appear weaker
- covering up inability to cope
- inattentiveness in class
- expectation of being 'spoon-fed' by teacher
- believing that there are right answers

- not bothering to plan essays
- not possessing or having access to essential reference sources: a good dictionary; a thesaurus; *Brewer's Dictionary of Phrase and Fable*; a history of English Literature; a dictionary of literary terms
- reliance on study guides and second-hand opinions
- submission of unchecked, illegible or incomplete work
- ignoring comments and advice on returned work
- lack of sleep and meals
- trying to get away with doing the minimum
- not having a clear idea of the course content and Assessment Objectives
- losing handouts and essays that will be needed for revision
- partial or superficial knowledge of the texts
- leaving essays to the last minute and rushing them

There are no short cuts to being a successful A-level Literature student. This means that copying from study guides, other students, your own previous essays, or from the internet is a counterproductive waste of time that could be much better spent studying the texts and forming your own opinions, working with the system rather than trying to defeat it. Good students talk in class; to paraphrase Milton, expressing opinions and receiving a response is knowledge in the making. Understanding is arrived at through contributing to discussion and supporting observations and viewpoints, not by passively accepting received wisdom. You can get out only what you put in; respond, and challenge in the classroom, and not only will you do well, you will actually enjoy the course.

Theory & background

LITERATURE

Studying English Literature

What is literature?

This is a huge question that does not have a clear-cut or commonly agreed answer among readers, writers, teachers or critics. Probably no one would disagree that it is composed of language and can be categorised as prose, poetry or drama, but that is about as far as agreement goes about an academic subject that has been called 'fuzzy'. One of the complications is that over the centuries it has become involved with the idea of national identity — and consequently with individual and group identity — as is evident from the fact that it is usually referred to at A-level and at university as studying or reading English rather than English Literature, and that the subject is hijacked by governments to indoctrinate the public or to prove the educational state of the nation.

Until the late nineteenth century (Oxford's first English degree course started in 1893) English Literature had been considered inferior to the classics, but its potential as a disseminator of moral and religious content — and therefore as a means of civilising native colonial populations, particularly in India — had been realised. It then became a recognised separate discipline, though it was still taught in schools by classicists for another half century. Novels were originally considered to be beneath poetry and not worthy of study, partly owing to the fact that the main readership of the novel, then and now, was female.

A lot can be learned, however, from thinking about the question, 'What is literature?' According to OCR, 'asking what makes a text "literary" is exactly the sort of question the new specifications should prompt from students' now that the inclusion of contexts and the questioning of traditional assumptions have broadened A-level courses, so that they encompass literary studies generally, rather than just particular works. Exam boards set texts and unseen passages that they consider to be of literary merit; your job is to identify and analyse what makes them so.

Definitions

(1) Look up the word 'literature' in several dictionaries and consider the similarities and differences between the definitions.

(2) Study the non-dictionary definitions of literature below and choose the best ones, considering your own experiences as a reader. Add examples of texts to each definition.

Literature:
- is 'news that stays news' (Ezra Pound)
- is writing in which every word matters
- is 'touched by the ice and fire of God' (George Steiner)

- teaches as well as entertains
- is a way of questioning what we know
- makes us more moral
- 'is the best that has been thought and said in the world' (Matthew Arnold)
- warns us of the future
- shows something that the microscope cannot; it is the bit left unexplained by science
- poses questions but does not answer them
- is where one and one make three
- is the real history you don't get in textbooks
- aids our understanding of humanity
- has universal applications and implications
- is the 'best chosen language' (Jane Austen)
- is the 'precious life-blood of a master spirit, embalmed and treasured' (John Milton)
- 'examines not the individual but the species' (Dr Johnson)
- 'is the pleasure of mind meeting mind' (Fay Weldon)
- is the supreme act of liberation in the modern world
- is designed to have designs upon us
- is an artifice to expose reality
- is writing that stands the test of time
- must say something original about life, not just for its own time, but for all time
- is that which is of permanent spiritual value
- is that which we want our children to read
- is the creative expression of the unique experience of certain highly gifted individuals
- embodies the fundamental truths of humanity
- is life processed for recognition inside a closed literary circuit
- is interested in means not ends
- imposes a discernible pattern and meaning on otherwise random experience

(3) Add one or more definitions of your own.

(4) Group these views and summarise their different viewpoints. Evaluate their validity.

(5) Do the above definitions suggest that literature must always be fiction? What is your opinion?

(6) Some of the definitions imply that art imitates life, whereas others seem to agree with Oscar Wilde that 'Life imitates Art'. What is your view on this matter? Give examples of particular texts as evidence.

(7) Jot down the names of a dozen writers of literature. Now count up the number of (a) women, (b) contemporary authors and (c) non-British writers in English. Consider the implications of your findings.

(8) List the texts you will be studying for AS/A2. Add the ones you read for GCSE. Include also the ones you did during KS3 as class readers and set texts. Count (a) the male and female authors and (b) the gender of the main character(s) in each text. What conclusions can be drawn?

The literary canon

The canon (Greek for 'rule', with a religious connotation) is the list of familiar and acceptable literary works imposed on society by the dominant institutions of the Western world, which T. S. Eliot described as the 'storehouse of Western values'. Apologists for the canon claim that we need a core of classics because they provide a common language, a shared area of experience, beyond that of television and newspapers. Furthermore, the canon, while transcending national boundaries, teaches us about the cultural history of the country we feel we belong to and has something positive to teach us about the humanity, tolerance and mutual respect required in a modern multicultural society. The canon, apologists argue, enshrines intrinsic literary value, and, far from being fixed and externally imposed, is the culmination of the choices of discerning readers over the centuries and is in a state of constant change.

The opposing view, first publicised by protests in the USA in the 1960s, is that the combined knowledge and experience of the canon cover a relatively small cultural area, impose a tyrannical conformity on literary studies and exclude 'otherness'. As Toni Morrison puts it, 'Canon building is empire building' and 'all the interests are vested'. There has been a questioning of the domination of syllabuses and publishers' lists by dead white European males (including the great god Shakespeare) and of practices that discriminate against women writers, such as the way literary prizes are awarded. Terry Eagleton argues that 'There is, in fact, no such thing as literature: literature is just the kind of writing which the cultural and academic establishments decide is literary' and that we should give equal attention to popular genres such as science fiction and soap opera. The literary canon could be accused of being self-fulfilling and self-perpetuating: books on A-level syllabuses stay in print, while others, which might be equally meritorious, fade away and cannot then be set by exam boards because they are out of print. Teachers choose the texts with which they are most familiar and for which there exists most support, and these choices reaffirm the canon.

Exam boards are indeed consistent in their inclusion of certain authors on their syllabuses, but recently more contemporary and female writers have appeared, along with post-colonial works and translations. This has made A-level text options more comprehensive and varied. Taste and fashion are other factors at work — for example, G. B. Shaw was once popular but is not nowadays. Conversely, texts acclaimed as modern classics may prove in retrospect to have been nine-day wonders — for example, it remains to be seen whether *Captain Corelli's Mandolin* retains its appeal over time. Again, there is a circular process involved, as exam boards, which are commercial, profit-making bodies, are likely to keep popular texts on their specifications longer and remove those for which there is little take-up in schools, regardless of the intrinsic merit of the text. As with other aspects of literature, an inclusion always involves an exclusion.

The canon, then, is being widened, despite the hostility of those who feel that 'More means worse' (Kingsley Amis) and that widening the canon dilutes it. OCR (Teacher Support 2000) says that the coursework texts 'do not have to be culled only from the canon…of texts traditionally set for A-level', but then admits to using the question-begging term 'literary texts' and quotes from the Subject Criteria that a literary text is defined as 'of sufficient substance to merit study at this level'. This takes us back to the question of 'What is literature?' Perhaps it would be easier to try to define what it is not.

Popular fiction

There is a grey area between literature and popular fiction across which people argue passionately for or against the inclusion of a particular author or work. This distinction is blurred further because some of the characteristics of trash or 'pulp' fiction seem to be shared not only by so-called literary texts but even by some of the 'great classics': being predictable and formulaic, and containing stereotyped characters and clichéd situations. Popular fiction is likely to offer, however, no more than a superficial and fleeting satisfaction to the reader, and no desire to reread the text. If the interest lies at the level of plot and is simply a matter of satisfying curiosity as to how the expected outcome (lovers' union, unveiling of murderer) will be arrived at, the novel has no depth to be returned to and can be instantly forgotten, since there is no stimulus to continue reflections beyond the last page.

Popular fiction, often criticised as valueless, has attractions for certain kinds of reader, or in certain contexts in which passive entertainment is more desirable than mental challenge. This one-dimensional blandness can be soothing and even addictive, as producers and marketers know very well. Many people use the word 'literary' pejoratively, to condemn what they perceive to be unacceptably elitist, 'highbrow' culture.

Quality fiction

Factors that determine whether a text is of 'sufficient substance and quality to merit serious consideration' (Qualifications and Curriculum Authority) could be whether or not it has a discernible structure separate from chronological narration; detailed or original characterisation; convincing dialogue; use of figurative language beyond clichéd similes; subtleties of meaning and layering; the power to engage the reader intellectually or emotionally: whether it shows as well as tells and whether it is memorable.

Fay Weldon describes thrillers and romances (*Letters to Alice*) as interchangeable and 'temporary things' that 'can never enlighten'. However, she says of Jane Austen's *Emma*, explaining why no one would dare to burn it, 'There is too much concentrated here: too much history, too much respect, too much of the very essence of civilization', which could be her definition of literature. A work of literature, as opposed to just a piece of fictional writing, has to work on many different levels simultaneously to be satisfying and edifying: character, plot, theme and imagery. The characters represent aspects of general humanity, as well as being individual creations. The plot conveys universal as well as particular dilemmas and conflicts. The themes are essential issues that remain of interest across historical, cultural and social divides. The imagery supports the themes and provides a pattern to give integrity to the work as a whole, and symbolically carries much of its meaning.

Though entertainment is a literary factor, and an important one, serious writers are didactic to some degree: writers write because they have something they wish to say, a message based on something they have perceived or experienced about the human condition and want to communicate to their readers. As Fay Weldon puts it (*Letters to Alice*):

> It [the novel] is the nearest we poor mortals can get to the Celestial City.... Writers create Houses of the Imagination, from whose doors the generations greet each other.... Some build because they need to, have to, live to, or believe they are appointed to, others to prove a point or to change the world.

The tendency to be tragic

The majority of texts that have earned the accolade of being labelled literature could be described as dealing with human suffering and, unlike popular fiction, they avoid a happy ending. Real experience does not live happily ever after; because loss and death are inevitable, life has to be acknowledged to be fundamentally and ultimately tragic. As Freud pointed out, the aim of life is death, and the death wish is endemic in literature.

Success and happiness are not only unconvincing but rather dull to read about; we are not really interested in well-behaved characters, but we are fascinated by badly behaved ones — with whom we can, of course, more readily identify. Evil has a dangerous charm (e.g. Milton's Satan and Shakespeare's Iago), whereas Dickens's and Austen's goody-goody heroines — the Doras and Biddies, Fannies and Eleanors — have always been attacked by critics and readers for their tedious virtuousness. Good is sameness, but evil takes many different forms, or as Tolstoy said in the opening sentence of *Anna Karenina*: 'Happy families are all alike; every unhappy family is unhappy in its own way.'

A matter of style

Another criterion for entry into the canon might be that of style, i.e. it is not what you say but how you say it.

> Across the crowded room he watched her ardently. She was arrestingly beautiful, like a wild cat. She smiled teasingly at him and he felt his heart leap dangerously.

This account of boy meets girl at party is in the 'Mills and Boon' style and is very different from the way in which the same actions would be described in a literary work, which would include detail and precise vocabulary, avoiding clichés and adverbs.

When you were slightly younger you may have read something that goes roughly like this:

> A new kid (girl) moves into town; there is something sinister about the house she moves into; terrible events happened there many years ago; she gets information from town residents regarded as eccentric; a bundle of letters/diary is found or a vision of some kind occurs; the girl is in danger and there is a chase-and-hide scene; a new friend (male) appears; a spooky location is the venue for a climactic showdown; there will be an injury and probably a hospitalisation; the menace is defeated.

It is actually a Point Horror synopsis, but could be the basis of a respectable literary work, depending on how it is fleshed out. The plot of *Wuthering Heights* could be made to sound similarly formulaic: romance to the death between a lady and a gypsy in a remote Gothic-horror house with devoted female servant and sinister old man, rivals and victims, violence and mystery. However, this does not convey the emotional power and reader engagement the novel generates through its structure, characterisation, dialogue, imagery, symbolism, atmosphere, social observation and irony.

Raymond Queneau wrote *Exercises de Style* (1947), in which he told the same story fragment in 99 different versions, including a diary entry in note form, one entirely in the passive voice, a police interrogation and a telegram. Some are recognisably literary, and others definitely not, so it would seem that form and style rather than content may be of paramount importance in determining what is literature, and there may be no new things to say, only new ways of saying them.

Controversies in literature

There are many bones of contention that arise in discussions about literary studies among authors, teachers, publishers, critics and readers, some of which are presented below.

- Can literature be rank-ordered? The growing number of literary prizes suggests that some people think that it can. Does it therefore follow that we have to ask whether Shakespeare is better than Jane Austen, whether poetry is better than prose or whether one sonnet is better than another? Can a modern playwright be compared to a Jacobean one? Can a Caribbean writer be compared to a Canadian one? Can a female writer be compared to a male one? Do we try to claim that one piece of music or a painting is better than another?

- What makes writing good or bad? The dispute about ranking literature is linked to the question of whether we can recognise good or bad writing. Is all vanity (self-financed) publishing by definition not of literary merit? But what of the acclaimed authors who had their submissions rejected many times by many publishers (including the Nobel prizewinner *Lord of the Flies*, which was turned down by 21 publishers and dismissed by one of them as 'Rubbish and dull. Pointless'). Can you recognise a greetings card rhyme, a pop song, a piece of rhyming doggerel out of context? Can you explain why they are not literary works? Below is an example of each of the aforementioned, plus verse by Wordsworth. Can you tell which is which? How do you know? (The sources of these extracts are given at the end of this section.)

Extract A
New neighbours have moved into next-door-but-one.
They have two nice children who seem lots of fun.
Their dog, too, is nice, but I get very tense
When it dirties my lawn, after jumping the fence.

Extract B
The cock is crowing,
The stream is flowing,
The small birds twitter,
The lake doth glitter,
The green field sleeps in the sun.

Extract C
Somehow it seems
That I can never say
All that I want to
On days like today,

I just can't express
All the love in my heart,
And the thankfulness, too,
No words can impart…

Extract D
We stumble in a tangled web,
Decaying friendships almost dead,
And hide behind a mask of lies.
We twist and turn and we avoid,
All hope of salvage now devoid
I see the truth inside your eyes.

Some academics in an American university all agreed that the following extract is the worst novel opening ever written. It is from *Paul Clifford*, by Edward George Bulwer-Lytton, 1830.

It was a dark and stormy night; the rain fell in torrents, except at occasional intervals when it was checked by a violent gust of wind that swept up the streets, for it is in London that our scenes lie, rattling along the housetops, and fiercely agitating the scanty flame of the lamps that struggled against the darkness.

But doesn't it sound a bit like Dickens? How do you know it isn't? And what exactly is 'wrong' with it? There are plenty of sentences in print that are similarly pretentious and prolix, with dangling parentheses, cliché and tautology. And not all of them are in trash romantic fiction.

- Does your view of a text change if you discover it is or is not, as you at first supposed, by someone famous, or vice versa? Critics from time to time ignore a work by a well-known writer using a false name. Doris Lessing demonstrated this point in 1983 when she published two novels under the pseudonym Jane Somers in order to highlight the plight of unknown novelists. Would Shakespeare still be Shakespeare if he were finally proved to be a less well-regarded contemporary? Or a woman? Is it acceptable for an author to pretend to be the other gender? Female authors have often had to pretend to be male, for sound reasons of defeating prejudice. There are few known examples of the reverse, such as that of the Anglican vicar who claimed to be an Asian adolescent female and was published by the feminist publisher Virago. When the deception was discovered, the book was promptly pulped. This reaction suggests that there are different standards and expectations for male and female writers and audiences.
- Is it possible for famous writers to have an 'off day' and write a terrible poem or piece of prose? Even fans of Wordsworth admit that he could; in addition to extract B on p. 16, there is this couplet from his poem called 'The Thorn'.

I've measured it from side to side:
'Tis three feet long, and two feet wide

- Is parody literature? It is argued that some genres can never be regarded as literature, and one of them is parody, on the grounds that it parasitically uses an existing text and with a negative purpose. Look at Lewis Carroll's 'You are old, Father William' (*Alice in Wonderland*) and then compare it to the object of its parody, Wordsworth's 'Resolution and Independence'. Can both be called literature; can one, or neither? Could advertising copy ever attain literary status? What about a political speech or a news report, or another genre that has a high fictional content?
- Can literature be created accidentally? Andrew Motion, poet laureate, thinks it can and sees poems everywhere: on sauce bottles, in public-service notices, in contents lists. Can literature be created through a hoax? What is your view of the following piece? It was written in 1944 by Australian James McAuley but attributed to a fictitious poet, Ern Malley, in order to reveal the philistinism of Australians.

   Night piece
   The swung torch scatters seeds
   In the umbelliferous dark
   And a frog makes guttural comment
   On the naked and trespassing
   Nymph of the lake

- Can there be poetic bits in a poem otherwise devoid of any literary merit? Is there anything in the above stanza that could be considered worthy of merit?
- Are some topics not fit for literary treatment? How do you feel about a poem about ironing, or one that begins 'Can I make it home, or do I shit/in the woods?' or 'They fuck you up, your mum and dad'.
- Oscar Wilde said, 'There is no such thing as an immoral book. Books are well written, or badly written.' Can a great book be written by an immoral writer? Can you value a book that expresses abhorrent views, such as Hitler's *Mein Kampf*? Where is the dividing line between literature and propaganda? What distinguishes the sensual from the pornographic?
- Books have power, or totalitarian regimes would not ban them. Salman Rushdie said that freedom of expression means freedom to offend. Is censorship anything more than ignorance, prejudice, taste or custom? Should texts have offensive elements removed to make them retrospectively politically correct? (For example, Graham Greene uses the word 'nigger' in his short story 'The Fallen Idol'.) Should Enid Blyton be banned on sexist grounds? Should Jane Austen be banned on classist grounds? Should anything be banned on any grounds?

Sources of the extracts on pp. 16–17

Extract A — vanity-published doggerel
Extract B — Wordsworth's 'Written in March'
Extract C — birthday-card message
Extract D — pop-song lyric (Savage Garden, 'A Thousand Words', 1997)

Role of the reader

Death of the author

Roland Barthes (1915–80) wrote an essay called 'The death of the author' in 1968 in which he declared that the presence of an author in a text is dead and buried, and he welcomed 'the birth of the reader'. Barthes argued that the explanation of a work is not to be found in the man or woman who produced it, or the narrator who speaks it, but in the reader who recreates the text every time it is read so that 'every text is eternally written here and now'. The author should not be seen as a god-like supreme creator, omniscient and omnipotent in controlling the puppet characters, as this implies that the author had a clear intention that the text embodies. Even if this were true, the authors are not available for comment in most cases, so we cannot appeal to them, alive or dead, as the final arbiters of all of a text's many and possibly contradictory meanings. And since the creative process is unconscious to a degree, they may well not know the answer. As D. H. Lawrence succinctly put it, 'Never trust the artist. Trust the tale.'

A text is a closed circle of meaning — not a reflection of the world it describes nor a reflection of its author's personality — and often one that was contradicted by the writer's own known views and practices. For example, in *Mansfield Park* the amateur theatricals are condemned, though Jane Austen herself was a keen participant. Even when writers have left extratextual evidence of their intentions, it does not mean they have achieved the effects they were seeking — for example, Milton's stated aim in *Paradise Lost* to 'justify the ways of God to man' — and they may well have conveyed others they were not even aware of. Words do not just do our bidding: unintended ambiguities occur, misleading impressions are given and readers have unpredictable personal associations with words, deriving from contexts outside the text. A statement of intention may be just as mystifying or as open to interpretation as the text itself, notoriously the case with Eliot's notes on 'The Waste Land', and Coleridge's marginal comments on 'The Rime of the Ancient Mariner'. Coleridge wrote 'Kubla Khan' under the influence of opium, so how meaningful is it to try to fathom his intention in that work? Why do different readers interpret the same text differently? Why do successive readings by the same reader of the same text sometimes produce different interpretations?

Birth of the reader

What we have on the page can always be interpreted in a variety of ways, so it is irrelevant to agonise about what the author really meant. This does not mean that readers can make a text mean anything they want, because some interpretations would be unsupportable and unsustainable. We can observe in Jane Austen's works the invisibility of the lower orders, the unconventional attitudes of Elizabeth Bennet and the friendship between Emma and Harriet, but we cannot plausibly claim that Jane Austen deliberately wrote communist, feminist or lesbian novels. False readings are those that ignore contradictory evidence in an attempt to impose one particular and extreme interpretation. Dickens was considered too bourgeois by the Soviet regime, yet too radical, with his liberal socialist attitudes, by many Victorians. Hardy's later novels shocked his reading public, but Lawrence, a fellow author, accused him of being too conventional. These examples of different readings show the range of possible responses and the importance of placing a work in its historical and social context.

Though there are wrong answers, i.e. unconvincing ones, there are no exclusively right answers, since readers are part of the process of constructing meaning. There is a boundary beyond which the author cannot go, and the very existence of the written text implies the absence and abdication of the writer. Authors shape words, but ultimately words are public property, and the reader, not the author, is the ultimate authority.

Intelligent reading

Knowing something about a literary text influences the way you respond and the way you feel about it. How your heart-strings or tears are jerked depends on knowing if what you are reading is true, false or spoof (extratextual knowledge). If you remember that even the most inspiring literature is artifice (metatextual knowledge), you will direct your roused feelings at real objects not fictional phantoms. How much pleasure you take from a literary text depends on knowing what aesthetic qualities to look for (intratextual knowledge). Reading literature is enhanced by knowing about other texts, traditions, contexts and genres (intertextual knowledge). Understanding how texts are presented, written, published, taught and read within naturalised networks of expectations is to rouse a protective suspicion of their possible propaganda effect (circumtextual knowledge).

(Andrew Stibbs, 'Precipitating Knowledge about Literature', *English & Media Magazine 37*, English & Media Centre, January 1998)

Readers are expected to think, not just to receive; as Jane Austen put it, writers do not write for 'dull elves without ingenuity'. The meaning of a text is contingent upon its similarities to and differences from other texts, and therefore it needs an active reader to decode it. But there is no such thing as a typical reader; everyone has culturally determined class, gender, racial and political associations and previous experiences of reading, which means they come to the text already encumbered with expectations about the genre, period, content and style. The following pointers deal with ways to keep the reading mind open:

- Although you may not have previously enjoyed a text by the same author, in the same genre, on the same subject, or in the same setting, a new set text should be given the benefit of the doubt. Try not to start with a prejudice against a text that prevents constructive engagement with it. Texts do not change, but readers do, and a book you considered unreadable at a certain age or stage in your life could become important to you later on, when you are ready for it. On the other hand, feel free to dislike a text, as long as you have considered why other readers value it and you can justify your dislike.

- Avoid the pitfall of the intentional fallacy, i.e. believing that the author had one specific and conscious aim and that you must find out what it was. Now that the work is in the public domain, intention is irrelevant as well as unprovable. However, do not go too far in the other direction and fall into the affective fallacy, or ignore the parts of the text that conflict with or are outside your own experience, or which you do not immediately relate to.

- Avoid leaping to a conclusion about a non-contemporary text by looking at it solely through modern eyes, and treat even contemporary texts with caution: the other gender, another nationality or someone of a different political persuasion may well view them very differently from you. Attitudes change over time; a modern list of the seven deadly sins, for instance, would be somewhat different from the original medieval one, and our attitude to war has changed fundamentally since Tennyson's 'The Charge of the Light Brigade'.

- Swallowing wholesale, and regurgitating in an exam, the views of any one critic, including your teacher, will give a biased response to text that fails to show awareness of other points of view or evidence of an informed personal response. Literary texts are complex, often ambiguous, and not susceptible to black-and-white interpretations; teachers and critics disagree with each other, and even with themselves over time. Thinking that there is only one view will prevent you from seeing the full range of possible interpretations.

- Be careful with the application of biographical knowledge: it can give support to your own interpretation but cannot be a substitute for your own observation and engagement with the text, and may be unhelpful or positively misleading. A homosexual poet could be writing about a heterosexual relationship. Biographical evidence is in itself only another text, equally open to interpretation by the reader, just as the subject's life story may have been misinterpreted by the biographer. This explains why biographies of the same subject tend to be surprisingly different in emphasis, and even fact.

- Characters are not, and are not meant to be, real people. A. C. Bradley was a Shakespeare scholar and is now largely discredited because he insisted on using this approach to fictional constructs. Kingsley Amis wrote an essay entitled 'What became of Jane Austen', arguing that Fanny Price and Edmund Bertram in *Mansfield Park* are 'insufferable prigs' and not the kind of people one could possibly invite to dinner. These are obviously unacceptable criteria for applying to character analysis and they ignore the context in which characters exist and have meaning through their relation to other characters.

Double vision

One of the common characteristics of literary texts is an inherent doubleness of vision, two ways of looking at something or two points from which to look. Life as we know it is full of paradox, coincidence and deceptive appearances. To capture and reflect these contradictory viewpoints of human experience (whereby we see ourselves and each other both through human eyes and as we would appear to gods looking down on us), literature employs modes and devices which deliberately keep both visions in the reader's mind, simultaneously or alternately, and which pit human aims against fate, destiny, providence, chance or what you will. Cosmic omniscience makes the dilemmas of individual humans seem trivial, whereas cosmic indifference to the plight of humanity enhances our tragic perspective.

Irony

Defined as the opposite of what was said, intended, expected or deserved, or as 'a way of taking people in' or 'a mockery of the fitness of things', what Hardy calls 'life's little ironies' (ironically, since they are in fact far from 'little') have featured in literature since it began. The word was introduced into common parlance in the eighteenth century, but it was used as a device by writers long before that (Plato's *Republic* first used the Greek word 'eironia' and exemplified it) and has played a leading role throughout the history of literature. In Chaucer's *Canterbury Tales* it is apparent that he is deliberately clashing opposing systems of thought — Christian and courtly love, noble and common attitudes — to point up their incompatibilities, defects and absurdities. Shakespeare dug irony deep into the foundations of his plots, character relationships and language. Until it was named, irony was an attribute of Fate or fickle Fortune, the woman with her wheel sending high to low, or of the Olympian gods, who mocked the hubris of ignorant mortals and enjoyed their punishment by Nemesis. Hardy continued the tradition of presenting irony in this way: 'The President of the Immortals…had ended his sport with Tess'. For some authors it is a way of commenting on the unjust workings of the universe; for others it is a weapon in their didactic or comic armoury.

The signs indicating that irony is present are sometimes subtle, causing difficulty to inexperienced readers. Conversely, a modern perspective can see it where it does not exist, as in Katharina's final speech in *The Taming of the Shrew*, where her acceptance of subservience is unlikely to be ironic given the prevailing views of women and the requirements of comedy. Excess and extremes can be warning indicators, as with Swift's immodestly boiled babies in *A Modest Proposal*. We usually acquire (for we cannot be taught) a sense of irony in our early teenage years, although a few never do and remain naive. As it is the mainspring of both comedy and tragedy, a student who is impervious to irony on both the large and small scale will be at a disadvantage in literary studies. Many a poem has been misread and misunderstood by a student failing to grasp that it is ironic, such as Browning's 'My Last Duchess'. You are advised to check all your set and unseen texts for irony. It is nearly always there in some form, either linguistic or situational, and can work intratextually, intertextually or contextually.

Sarcasm

There is sometimes a confusion in usage between the terms ironic and sarcastic. The former, consciously or unconsciously, calls attention to the doubleness of something, but is not an aim in itself. The latter is a description of a bitter remark whose purpose is specifically to wound or cause offence to someone. An ironic tone of voice is amused or pained; a sarcastic one is scornful. There may be some overlap between the two in dialogue, as when someone says both ironically and sarcastically, 'You're a fine one to talk', but there is still a distinction to be made between the device (irony) and the intention (sarcasm). One cannot be unknowingly sarcastic.

Satire

Satire is also linked to and sometimes confused with irony. But satire is a genre whose purpose is to expose something or someone to ridicule and contempt, whereas irony is just one of the devices that may be employed, others being hyperbole or rhetoric, for instance. Authors who viciously attack institutions and personalities in the hope of reform, such as Jonathan Swift, are known as satirists, whereas those who mock human nature without suggesting anything can be done about it, such as Chaucer and Jane Austen, are described as ironists.

Stereotypes

Normally found in comedy, stereotyped characters require the reader to accept that they are individuals in terms of the plot but also representatives of their social, national or personality types, and as such they are being mocked — for instance, Jane Austen's vicars, Mr Elton and Mr Collins.

Caricature

As in political cartoons, a caricatured figure in a literary text is immediately recognisable, yet also known to be a gross exaggeration and distortion of a character's appearance, behaviour or speech for comic or satirical effect. Dickens created many memorable caricatures — for example, Scrooge and Pumblechook.

Allegory

Animal Farm, *Gulliver's Travels* and *Alice in Wonderland* are examples of well-known texts that work on two levels at once, in which the apparently innocent plot disguises the subversive message in order to protect the writer. Allegorical texts refer obliquely to nonfictional people, incidents, beliefs and practices, requiring the reader to decode characters and events in order to recognise their political and sociological significance and the satirical targets of the work.

Comic irony

Irony has been used as a didactic tool since *Aesop's Fables* were written in the sixth century BC. Fables and fairy tales originated as genres for teaching morals concerning human behaviour, and they work by using the concept described in Hamlet as being 'hoist with your own petard', i.e. being ironically defeated by your own weapon turned back on yourself. When humans and gods can reconcile their visions and agree on a happy outcome, comic resolution and harmony are achieved. In comedy the faults of the villains must be fittingly punished by the end of the narrative, and the virtues of the others rewarded, reversing the previous balance of power within the text. There is a justice in this that readers find satisfying as it gives the impression, at least temporarily, that we live in a moral universe where everyone gets their just deserts and that it is therefore worth following the rules. Ironically, we expect all literary texts to have a moral ending, although we know that this runs counter to real experience.

Tragic irony

When the contrary plans or indifference of the superior agency defeat the desires of frail humanity, we have a tragic outcome involving irreparable loss. The irony lies in the unjust punishment of innocent characters in order that the wicked ones get their comeuppance, and in the way that heroes are brought down by a fault or misjudgement that is outweighed by their many excellent qualities, but which nonetheless destroys them because of a particular adverse set of circumstances. There are other ironies involved in tragedy that are to do with the timing of the plot, misjudgement of character by other characters and the unfortunate role of external agents, such as the witches in *Macbeth*.

Dramatic irony

This is a device used in both comic and tragic drama, whereby the audience is aware of elements in the situation of which one or more of the characters involved are unaware (e.g. Duncan's praising of Macbeth's pleasant castle), which lends added humour or pathos to impending events. This superior knowledge implicates the audience in the play's action and fosters sympathetic engagement with the ignorant and innocent characters.

Ambiguity

Ambiguity is the existence, deliberately or not, of one or more possible alternative meanings. According to the critic William Empson (*Seven Types of Ambiguity*, 1930), it is the 'rock and shifting sand' of critical appreciation. A poet himself, Empson pointed out that in poetry particularly (because of its compression and where associations, density and layering are more important than clarity) we must watch out for ambiguity of different types — linguistic, imagistic, conceptual — to tease out wider and deeper resonances and meanings, and be able to appreciate simultaneously alternative interpretations.

Ambivalence

It is common for a reader to hold a double view of a character or theme in a literary work, whereby behaviour is both admired and condemned (as with Iago, for instance). An issue can be seen from two conflicting viewpoints, so that no definite opinion or acceptable moral position can easily be arrived at. This is usually caused by an ambivalence in the author's attitude to or presentation of a character, event or dilemma, as betrayed by use of language of narrative voice. As D. H. Lawrence pointed out, 'It is the job of art to pose questions not to answer them', and therefore the sowing of doubt and contradiction is often deliberate — to reflect the complexity of human beings and the situations they find themselves in.

Intertextuality

For an appreciation of intratextual and contextual irony, students need to know the work in question and its social climate. A wider knowledge, however, is necessary for a recognition of intertextual irony, including not only generic codes but specific previous works. Throughout the history of literature, texts have been predicated upon former versions of the same story or dependent upon them for interpretation. For instance, Stoppard's *Rosencrantz and Guildenstern Are Dead* would be unintelligible to an audience unfamiliar with *Hamlet*, Jean Rhys's *Wide Sargasso Sea* presupposes a prior reading of *Jane Eyre*, and Walcott's *Odyssey* and Tennyson's 'Ulysses' require at least a passing acquaintance with the plot of Homer's epic. While considering a later version the reader has to hold in mind the original to be aware of the ironies created by the comparison.

Romantic versus classical

These two systems of thought can be said to have used the Western literary canon as their battleground for many centuries. They are fundamental oppositions in literature (and in the other arts) and can be used to distinguish and discriminate between characters, actions, attitudes, settings and, most importantly, moral stance. The only thing they have in common is a focus on humanity and a nostalgia for the past (though for different eras of it). Earlier literary periods could be characterised as predominantly Romantic or classical in outlook, but since the middle of the nineteenth century, society and literary genres have become increasingly complex and such simple ways of ordering the world can no longer be applied. You can therefore expect both legacies to be present in your literary studies, either in different works of the same period or as a cause of conflict within the same work.

Classical

The term 'classical' embraces nostalgia for and emulation of the literary practices and social values of Greek and Roman antiquity. These include a belief that only the intellect can raise us above an existence otherwise indistinguishable from that of animals, who live by their instincts and appetites. Elegance of expression and control of form are civilised virtues, and universal concerns are more enduring and important than those pertaining to the individual. As Dr Johnson said, 'the business of a poet…is to examine not the individual but the species…he does not number the streaks of the tulip'. The aim of classical writing is usually didactic rather than affective, hence the tendency towards the well-tried formulae of satirical or polemical essay, ode and (mock) epic, which favour rhetoric, conventional imagery and abstract concepts. It is also associated with comedy, in which restraint, balance and harmony are paramount considerations. Classical texts do not normally include references to animals, women, children or peasants, as the proper study of man is man as a political animal, and his role in the community and public life. Their contexts, therefore, are usually urban and contain the dialogue and debate of educated discourse. Many works of the late seventeenth and eighteenth centuries are in the classical mode, such as those of Milton, Dryden, Swift and Pope.

Romantic

The Romantic period (roughly 1775–1840) heavily influenced subsequent literature and thus its concerns may seem more familiar, accessible and contemporary. Romanticism's chief tenets are the importance of childhood, passion, the individual, the personal, love and nature. Romantic texts remind us of the fairy-tale tradition we have been familiar with since bedtime stories. According to this approach to life, feelings are to be trusted rather than thoughts, and impulses followed are safer than rules obeyed. Romantics champion rebellion, nonconformity and the cause of the little man against the system. They prefer to be outdoors and revere nature as a divine force; those who cut themselves off from their natural roots in the countryside will perish spiritually. Romantics believe that not everything can or should be explained by logic or science, and that some mystery should be left in the world because the creative human imagination needs to feed on magic and fantasy. Because everything is in a state of flux — and therefore happiness, youth, beauty, innocence and emotions are ephemeral — it is necessary to live by the Latin proverb '*carpe diem!*' ('seize the day!') and spontaneously snatch fleeting pleasure from the jaws of time. Because of the inevitability of loss, pain, physical decay and old age the Romantic mode is a tragic one, often involving someone dying young.

The arts play an important role in the Romantic world view, since for them music and poetry are statements of independence capable of evoking the deepest emotion and of providing inspiration to others. Romantics look back to the medieval world as a way of defining the experiences of humans in relation to the natural environment, which is both sustaining and hostile, and to their tempestuous and traumatic relationships with others within the family and the social structure. They are more concerned with sensitivity of perceptions than with their formal expression, hence the tendency of Romantic works to be incomplete or to shift in form or tone within the same text — the emotions and moods of the moment are paramount. Life and the affairs of the heart are too serious for humour; metaphors and neologisms are favoured, as true flights of imagination, over anything contrived or traditional, which includes similes.

Opposing forces

Below are examples of the classical/Romantic divide:

- fancy/imagination
- sun/moon
- static/kinetic
- company/solitude
- head/heart
- public/private
- order/chaos
- marriage/love
- reason/instinct

- sense/sensibility
- restraint/indulgence
- moderation/extravagance
- mechanical/organic
- duty/desire
- tame/wild
- regular/irregular
- conscious/unconscious
- nurture/nature

Works across a range of literary periods examine the tension between classical and Romantic, such as Stoppard's *Arcadia*, Milton's *Paradise Lost* (with Satan as Romantic hero) and the poetry of Tennyson.

Many famous literary characters can be described as either Romantic or classical according to their temperament, and the conflicts within relationships and plots are often caused by this fundamental incompatibility, such as that between Clym and Eustacia in *The Return of the Native*, and the married couple in Kate Chopin's *The Awakening*. Nearly all genres of narrative fiction, from Westerns to soap operas, fabliaux to fairy tales, rely on the convention of there being two opposite types of people to become rivals and make the choice of partner a dilemma for heroes and heroines: Marian in *The Go-Between* has Ted and Hugh; Maire in *Translations* has Manus and Yolland; Cathy in *Wuthering Heights* has Heathcliff and Edgar. This dilemma has become known as the love triangle and is the staple of many plots: the wrong choice can be rectified in a comedy, but in a tragedy there is no second chance after choosing wrongly the first time.

Eponymous heroes/heroines are more likely to be Romantic, and these tend to be the characters whom readers remember and with whom they identify, rather than their more sober and less exciting classical counterparts. Evil and unhappiness are more fascinating and give rise to more response and debate than goodness and stability. Though they are beloved — unlike their sensible, restrained rivals — the author (acting on behalf of society) tends to dispose of the threat posed by unorthodoxy and extremism by putting the Romantic heroes/heroines to death or allowing them to die. (Authors who were themselves nonconformist suffered exile and the suppression or condemnation of their books, e.g. Byron, James Joyce, D. H. Lawrence.) Classical characters usually survive, lacking the passion and impetuousness that would lead them into fatal danger. Reader sympathies depend on the positioning by the author, so Romantics can be presented as dangerous, self-indulgent troublemakers by Jane Austen, although in the majority of works they attract reader sympathy for their sensitivity and frustration.

Some leading characters do not fit neatly into either category and contain the conflict within themselves, which is itself the root of their dissatisfaction and the cause of their downfall, since they are torn apart by these irreconcilable forces. Their sticky end is suicide or a symbolic manifestation thereof, as with Shakespeare's Hamlet and Antony, and Hardy's Tess and Jude.

Romantic heroes and heroines

The youthful Romantic hero and heroine were derived from medieval court life, as depicted in the Arthurian legends. Although they span many centuries, they have changed very little, even in outward appearance. Heroes have an exotic or aristo-cratic name and are tall, dark, handsome, sensitive, intelligent, witty, moody, athletic, rebellious, impetuous, seductive, strong, bold, charming, idealistic and independent. They are horsemen and swordsmen, or the equivalent, and lovers. Their job is to save their country, comrades and helpless females, from themselves or their abusers, through brave and dangerous exploits. Heroines have foreign names (usually three syllables ending in '-a', e.g. Estella), are beautiful, long-dark-haired, unconventional, creative, emotional, proud, wilful, secretive, dependent, long-suffering and misunderstood. They provoke envy in other women, desire in men, and await deliverance by a knight in shining armour.

The dividing line between Romantic hero and villain or heroine and *femme fatale* is a narrow one, hence the deception and disillusionment inherent in many Romantic literary works whereby a false hero/heroine is confused with a true one (e.g. Wickham with Darcy in *Pride and Prejudice*). These Romantic stereotypes were the staple of characterisation until the early twentieth century, since when most authors have tried to steer clear of them (now relegated to the realms of pulp fiction) and instead to create antiheroes and antiheroines, protagonists who combine a mixture of vices and virtues, attractive and unattractive qualities, i.e. real human beings rather than anachronistic archetypes. However, Romeos and Juliets, Robin Hoods and Maid Marians still live on in the film industry (e.g. Bond films) and some contemporary literary works, such as *Captain Corelli's Mandolin*, still draw heavily upon them.

Comedy and tragedy

The terms comedy and tragedy both derive from village life and ritual celebrations in ancient Greece. Though originally drama terms, they later became applicable to poetry and prose. The word 'comedy' comes from the Greek '*komoidia*', meaning 'village song', and signifies a satisfactory outcome. A comic resolution involves lovers being reconciled amid feasting, joking, singing and dancing, all of which represent harmony. Tragedy, which originated in Dionysiac choral song in the Greece of the fifth century BC, literally means 'goat song' ('*tragoidia*') — a possible reference to the sacrifice of innocent creatures to propitiate the gods. You need to be aware that these literary terms have more specific meanings than those in everyday use: comedy may not be funny, and tragic means much more than just sad.

It is generally held that comedy satisfies the reader or audience not only because a positive outcome is reassuring, but also because we can feel safe and relieved that we are not involved in the misfortunes of others. Whereas tragedy makes us feel pity for the suffering of the characters and a fear that it could happen to us, we feel sufficiently emotionally distant and indifferent to the plight of characters who are being humiliated, injured or baffled in comedy to be able to feel superior to them rather than want to identify with them. However, though it may keep us sane, comedy also keeps us in a state of social conformity; we enjoy nothing more than to laugh with others, we fear nothing more than to be laughed at ourselves.

Tragedy, on the other hand, is about daring to be different, which provokes the wrath and punishment of the gods, and of society. In tragedy, which traditionally involves multiple deaths — some undeserved — the events seem directed by fate, which overrules the intentions and desires of the human victims, creating a sense

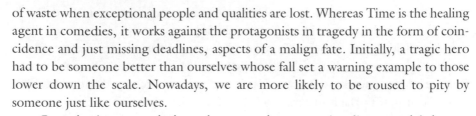

of waste when exceptional people and qualities are lost. Whereas Time is the healing agent in comedies, it works against the protagonists in tragedy in the form of coincidence and just missing deadlines, aspects of a malign fate. Initially, a tragic hero had to be someone better than ourselves whose fall set a warning example to those lower down the scale. Nowadays, we are more likely to be roused to pity by someone just like ourselves.

Comedy aims to teach through an appeal to our rationality; tragedy's lessons are delivered through the evocation of an emotional response. Both genres make use of irony. In some texts, including Shakespeare's tragedies, comic incidents and conversations occur although the work is predominantly serious in mood. The juxtaposition of horror and pathos with moments of light relief creates an ironic contrast that highlights the tragic elements and draws attention to the contradictions of human experience and perception. They also allow the audience/readers to be tricked into hoping for a better outcome than the one they are going to get, which makes the reapplied tension even more effective, and the outcome more ironic.

If your current coursework or exam set text was written before the late twentieth century, it is likely to be clearly definable as a comedy or a tragedy. However, it is more difficult to tell with later works (e.g. a play by Stoppard); the work may even be an amalgam of both, like *Captain Corelli's Mandolin*, whose outcome is arguably comic, but only just. Some of Shakespeare's comedies are called 'dark' or problem comedies, because the mood is sombre and there is fatal danger present, e.g. *Measure for Measure* and *Twelfth Night*, and the comic resolution of *The Tempest* is uneasy. It is usually possible, however, to tell from the beginning of a text, even before character and plot have been introduced, whether it will have a comic or tragic resolution. Setting, atmosphere, diction, tone and, in particular, imagery are early indicators.

Humour, or black humour, can be created by treating a serious incident (e.g. a lovers' reunion or the death of a relative) as amusing, thereby undermining the expectations of the audience/reader. Likewise the treatment of a trivial event as tragic can have the same effect. In both cases incongruity and irony are present, and viewpoint has to be controlled by the writer to prevent reader sympathy being evoked, which would then introduce a tragic perspective to cancel the humour. Postmodern texts, such as the plays of Pinter and Beckett, often use black humour to defamiliarise text and raise questions about narrative codes and audience conditioning.

Whether writers choose to write in comic or tragic mode depends on various factors: their natural inclination, temperament and philosophy of life; childhood and other personal experiences; the particular topic or source story that fascinates them; the tastes of their audience. Some writers progress from comedy to tragedy, though rarely the other way round. As writers develop and mature, they tend to become less optimistic as a result of direct experience of disappointment and loss, as was true of Thomas Hardy.

Tragedy best suits the taste of post-Romantic audiences and has attracted the majority of literary criticism. Comedies tend to be treated as lightweight and appropriate for less mature audiences by both the media and school curricula. 'This world is a comedy to those that think, a tragedy to those that feel' (Horace Walpole). We live in a sensuous and anti-intellectual age; emotions, desires and individualism are allowed free rein and applauded, whereas thought, mental discipline and community spirit are considered difficult and are undervalued. Henry Ford said 'Thinking is the hardest thing that anyone can do', whereas feeling is easy, passive and automatic. We can identify easily with the downfall of tragic heroes and enjoy the philosophising that goes with a recognition of the abstract concepts of irony, fate and hubris, which are inseparable from the tragic mode. Although we also enjoy humour, comedy as a genre is less convincing than tragedy in its insistence that 'all's well that ends well' and that everything can be solved with a kiss, a song and a good dinner. Our own experience tells us differently, and as death is the inevitable end of life, no amount of comedy can change the true nature of things, which is tragic. As Freud pointed out, the aim of life is death, and the death wish is endemic in literature. Tragedy is more interesting and varied than comedy because 'Happiness writes white' (Dostoyevsky) and 'Happy families are all alike; every unhappy family is unhappy in its own way' (Tolstoy).

Myths and symbols

According to Jung's theory of the 'collective unconscious', literary symbols derive from the common experience of primitive society rather than from the personal experience of the individual. Western literature has descended from three main sources: the Bible, classical mythology and medieval fairy tales. This means that archetypal characters and events have become part of literary tradition and are instantly recognisable as such in a variety of genres, such as the father figure and the *femme fatale*, transformations and trials. There is also a fixed set of symbols that can be used by writers as a kind of shorthand because of their traditional associations with all three sources, such as the apple. The same myths and symbols occur in art and music and have been transferred into the cinema.

Originally these characters, events and symbols were a way of explaining the eternal verities and of finding a concrete correlative for an abstract concept, and they still serve the same purpose of imposing a discernible pattern and meaning on otherwise random experience. The battle between good and evil — internationally, nationally, within the community, family and individual psyche — is as much the stuff of literature now as it was in Homer's day. Therefore, the same myths and symbols are still relevant and the shorthand is still useful and can be plundered whenever a metaphor is needed. (Contemporary politicians are defined as hawks or doves, for instance.)

Myths

In addition to the myths linked to momentous events in theology, such as the Creation, the Flood and the Apocalypse, there are specific mythical characters that have captured the imagination of writers of many generations and cultures, and are still being 'recycled' up to the present day. Homer's Odysseus is one of them, and he has given us works as diverse as Tennyson's 'Ulysses' and James Joyce's *Ulysses*. The story of Odysseus has given literature the recurring features of the long-lost wanderer returning to a much-missed homeland, the mariner storyteller, the disguised lover and the soldier who did great deeds in the war. Icarus is another mythological archetype, the overreacher who flew too near the sun. The Bible has given us Samson, David and Judas: the man of superhuman strength, betrayed by a woman, who pulls down the pillars; the little man who dared take on the giant; and the traitor. From folklore we have the wise, old wizard figure Merlin and the mistreated servant Cinderella, who have reappeared countless times in later works and are still popping up in children's fiction. Modern soap opera is as dependent as Shakespeare's plays on myths that represent breakdown and regeneration, death and birth.

Below are some examples of typical elements of plot and characterisation used in texts of any genre:

- helpless maiden rescued by brave prince
- being granted a wish as a reward
- sea voyage to a new country and a new life
- slaying of a monster against all the odds
- lost children surviving without adults
- long-lost relative, believed dead, turning up unannounced
- recovery from being ill/wounded and on the brink of death
- poor orphan revealed to be rich
- overreacher aspires too high and is punished
- former friends become sworn enemies, or vice versa
- a promise has to be kept whatever the cost
- a strange experience in the woods
- a coward or weakling becomes brave and strong
- an evil character has a change of heart
- a stranger arrives in town and poses a threat
- something dangerous is unwittingly let loose
- a harsh parent learns to be gentle
- a defeated team becomes victorious
- siblings have totally opposite personalities

Symbols

The most common symbols in literature are the four elements: earth, air, fire and water. They are primeval, cosmological and related to creation and end-of-the-world myths. They are also the constituents of the planet Earth and of the human body, according to the medieval world view. They are part of our collective unconscious and do not need to be explained. Because of their ambiguity, depending on scale, writers can use them to represent either a redeeming or a destructive force in each case: water is cleansing or cataclysmic; air is refreshing breeze or howling gale; earth is growth or grave; fire is hearth or holocaust. Many literary works in all periods, including poems, make symbolic use of the four elements, and some refer to them in their titles too.

Drawing from the three literary sources, writers use certain animals and plants as symbols, to evoke a strong reader reaction (positive or negative), or to represent a quality: fox is sly, lion is strong, rose is romantic etc. The more these symbols are used in literature, the more they reinforce their symbolic values. Even the letter 'S' is enough to suggest snake, serpent, Satan and all things hissingly evil. Likewise a limited group of colours can be used as immediately recognisable codes in literature: e.g. red for danger, white for purity, black for death. (L. P. Hartley's *The Go-Between* relies upon this triple chromatic symbolism.) Numbers are likely to be three (trinity, bears, wishes, witches, goddesses), or nine (3 × 3), seven (dwarves, deadly sins, ages of man, lean years) or twelve (Apostles, tribes of Israel, the Arthurian legends and the clock). There are also key objects — and a key is one of them — used as symbols in literature; and certain places (e.g. gardens and islands), features of landscape (e.g. cliffs and rivers) and weather (especially storms) all contribute to the creation of atmosphere and expectation because of their traditional associations.

The words below are examples of literary symbols. We know this because your response will be the same as that of other readers in not only responding to the word/thing with either a clearly positive or negative reaction, but also being able to describe exactly what the connotations and associations (derived from the three sources of literature) are:

milk	rainbow	lamb	lily
honey	castle	swan	harp
wine	wolf	owl	gold
bread	goat	raven	heart
moon	cat	eagle	star

Some symbols are usefully dual-purpose, e.g. bed (marriage and death), blood (life and violence) and eyes (love and tyranny). Because of the literary attractions of irony (see 'Double vision' on p. 22), these, in addition to the four elements, are the symbols that you are most likely to come across. Some genres — horror and detective novels, for instance — deliberately reverse the accepted symbolism, so that a charming child or amiable old lady turns out to be the fiend or the murderer. The shock of the dénouement relies on our having been conditioned as readers/viewers not to suspect them, because in other genres such characters would symbolise innocence.

Certain events and actions, and their opposites, are also symbolic across a range of literary genres. The following are examples of those that would leave the reader in no doubt of their implications for the character performing them:

- lying awake
- unravelling a piece of needlework
- burying something
- descending
- getting lost
- lighting a candle

It has been claimed that there is nothing new in literature — only new ways of saying the same old thing — and that all stories can be reduced to the 15 archetypal plots listed below. For each of these, suggest the name of a relevant fairy tale, classical myth or Bible story, and give examples of novels or films that have used them.

- A baffling mystery is finally solved with help from an unlikely source.
- Dangers are overcome and the land is saved because of cooperation.
- A trial ends with a just outcome thanks to last-minute extra evidence.
- Boy meets girl but there is an obstacle to their love.
- A quest is finally successful because of a lucky break.
- The deceiver is deceived and gets a comeuppance.
- An escape/rescue is planned and carried out successfully, with setbacks.
- Outsiders cause problems and then return to where they came from.
- A triangular love story is finally resolved with a death.
- Ghosts have to be laid to rest so that peace and normality can be restored.
- Rags to riches: a poor boy or girl works hard and makes good.
- Riches to rags: a pampered person falls on hard times and is the better for it.
- Growing up: innocence learns painfully through experience.
- A victim plans and waits for an opportunity for revenge but then shows mercy.
- A despised person is re-evaluated after saving the community.

Are there any more archetypal plots?

Medieval and Elizabethan world view

The Elizabethans inherited a set of assumptions about the universe and man's position in it from the medieval Church, and Shakespeare examines many concepts that are also referred to in Chaucer's works. To put Chaucer's poetry and Shakespeare's plays in their social and historical contexts, you need a basic understanding of the prevailing taboos and beliefs, customs and superstitions. However, you need also to be aware that both authors are often questioning these views rather than simply endorsing them, and that different attitudes are expressed by different characters within the same work.

The Elizabethans inherited from medieval theology the concept of a hierar-chical Great Chain of Being, on which every creature appears in its ordained position on a ladder descending from God through angel, king, man and woman (in that order) to animal, vegetable and finally mineral. It is necessary to know this belief in a divine order to appreciate why women should not dictate to men (Lady Macbeth's crime), why ordinary mortals should not aspire to be king (Macbeth's crime) and why it was believed that failure to apply reason reduced humans to the animal state of being governed by appetite and instinct (the crime of too many to mention). In Shakespeare, a human who falls below the level of man into the realm of bestiality is labelled a monster. Conversely, any attempt to rise above one's proper station on the ladder resulted not only in the offender being cast down several rungs (Satan fell from angel to reptile) but also in disorder and violent consequences being inflicted upon adjacent parties and the surrounding social fabric. The table below shows this hierarchy and the associated properties of each level.

Item	Properties
God	Reason, Movement, Life, Existence
Angels	Reason, Movement, Life, Existence
Man	Reason, Movement, Life, Existence
Animals	Movement, Life, Existence
Plants	Life, Existence
Inanimate matter	Existence

The failure of reason was considered to be the cause of the Fall of Man (Adam allowed his love for Eve to overrule his better judgement and obedience to God), and from the Middle Ages onwards it was believed to be dangerous to let reason be dominated by passion. Characters in Chaucer and Shakespeare who become uncontrollably emotional are heading for a fall, as their intellect is what makes them human (superior to beasts) and keeps them sane. Othello gives way to his wrath — 'My blood begins my safer guides to rule' (II.3.200) — and this is the downward turning point for him. In a state of heightened passion, such as anger and jealousy, mistakes are made, impulses are activated without sufficient reflection to moderate them, and people are no longer in control of themselves or of the situation.

The idea of harmony through bonds and 'understood relations' (*Macbeth*) was very important to the Elizabethans, who had a terror of anarchy, chaos and a return to the civil wars of the period prior to the Tudor settlement and the largely peaceful reign of Elizabeth. In Shakespeare's plays, harmony, which is the principle governing

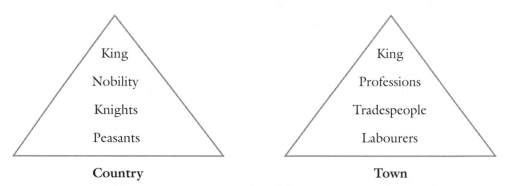

the stars and nature (referred to as 'the music of the spheres'), is expressed as music, dance, feasting and love. The publication of Thomas More's *Utopia* in 1516 encouraged speculation about the possibility of an ideal world that could be created or was already in existence somewhere as yet undiscovered. Elizabethans were particularly interested in the search for the perfect form of government, and many plays contain speeches on this topic, e.g. Gonzalo's in *The Tempest*. The word 'utopia' means 'no place', however, and it was already feared that it was an impossible ideal in a fallen world.

The view of kingship explored in Shakespeare is how semi-divinity — being nearer to heaven — can be reconciled with being a father, brother, husband and man. Kings have duties, such as administering justice as God's temporal power on earth, which require sound judgement and cannot morally be neglected or abdicated, but which may conflict with other relationships. This is central to an understanding of the problems of King Lear and Henry IV. Because a king was believed to be divinely appointed, the killing or usurping of a king was a heinous offence that had devastating consequences for the state.

Medieval society was organised hierarchically according to what is known as the feudal system, in which everyone had an exact degree, i.e. a position, on the social scale as either an urban or rural dweller. Women did not feature as they were only adjuncts to the men whom they married and did not have jobs, education, skills or property rights. The question asked by Chaucer and by Shakespeare is whether social rank (or lack of it in the case of bastards) determines moral status, i.e. whether nobility and gentility are the preserve of the higher orders only.

Country	Town
King	King
Nobility	Professions
Knights	Tradespeople
Peasants	Labourers

The microcosm/macrocosm medieval theory still influential in Shakespeare's time was that the king (ruled by reason) was the head and centre of the body politic, so that if anything untoward happened to him or his sanity, the consequences would ripple outwards like a stone thrown into a pond, causing a breakdown of normal relations at every level: family, court, state, planet. In Shakespeare, storms and tempests are symbolic of disruption in nature caused by human transgression of the natural order. Thus, humans represented the world in miniature, which led to a belief in a correspondence between the natural elements and the composition of the human body, connected by astrology, which professed to interpret personal and political events according to the movements of the stars. This is much mentioned in Shakespeare's plays, e.g. *Romeo and Juliet*.

The medieval world view still being given some credence in the late sixteenth century was that just as the universe was composed of the four elements, so humans were composed of four humours related to the elements. An imbalance of the mixture of humours created temperament and explained the differences in human personality. Hamlet, for instance, is a melancholy type, and the play is dominated by earth imagery; Chaucer's Reeve is a 'choleric man'. The table below lists the types of elements and humours and their associated qualities. Each element was also believed to correspond to a planet and a season.

Element	Planet	Season	Qualities	Humour	Personality
Fire	Mars	Summer	Hot and dry	Yellow bile (spleen)	Choleric (angry)
Air	Jupiter	Spring	Hot and wet	Blood (heart)	Sanguine (cheerful)
Water	Moon	Winter	Cold and wet	Phlegm (brain)	Phlegmatic (calm)
Earth	Saturn	Autumn	Cold and dry	Black bile (liver)	Melancholic (sad)

The ubiquitous presence of the word 'nature' in Elizabethan literature, in addition to imagery pertaining to it and arguments concerning it, stems from the contemporary debate about the definition of nature, which has contradictory aspects: the benevolent and harmonious, reflecting a divine order, and the wild and violent, symptomatic of punishment and breakdown. Shakespeare plays with the paradox of the existence of unnatural monsters (such as Lear's daughters Goneril and Regan), who could have been bred only by nature and must, therefore, be natural in some sense. His plays also examine closely the concept of human nature — 'kind' or 'unkind'? — and its relationship with nature as a whole.

External appearance was believed by many in the ages of Chaucer and Shakespeare to be an indicator of what lay within, i.e. goodness or evil. This legacy is still with us, whereby beauty and whiteness are associated with fair, and ugliness and blackness with foul. A physical deformity was considered to be the devil's mark and enough to condemn many women to being burned at the stake as witches. Shakespeare's Richard III is vilified because of his deformities, which are his excuse for behaving vilely. Appearance versus reality is a central issue in many of Shakespeare's plays, tormenting the heroes and permeating the language, as the Elizabethans began to question the reliability of outward signs.

Evil spirits were believed to be ever within earshot and on the watch for an opportunity to corrupt and snatch a human soul from the pathway of righteousness. Only constant vigilance, fasting, prayer and good thoughts could ensure that evil would keep its distance. Characters in Shakespeare who are foolish, hubristic or tempted enough to invoke spirits from murky hell (such as Macbeth and his wife, and Othello) to help them commit foul deeds are inviting their own damnation. It was also thought possible to be tricked into carrying an evil creature, disguised as a fair one, across the threshold into one's house (a fear still observed in the tradition of the groom carrying the bride into their new home to protect her from evil spirits lying in wait under the threshold), with the same dire consequences. The fear of hell so apparent in the works of Shakespeare and his fellow playwrights arises from a contemporary conviction that there was such a place, below ground, inhabited by tormented souls (victims of violent death without absolution) that walked the earth between midnight and dawn, before returning to their graves. In addition to super-natural evil in the form of ghosts, spirits and witches, Chaucer's and Shakespeare's contemporaries believed in diabolic possession and the incarnation of the devil and his agents in human form.

The seven deadly sins of the medieval Church were pride, envy, gluttony (food), lechery (lust), avarice (money), wrath (anger) and sloth (laziness). These vices, which can be identified in literary works until well into the nineteenth century, were the foundation of morality in the medieval and Elizabethan periods. (They feature as a masque in *Doctor Faustus*, for instance.) Shakespeare has them hovering in the background of his works as a means of judging the transgressions of protag-onists and villains (e.g. Leontes is guilty of wrath, Iago of envy, Shylock of avarice). These mortal sins, most of which were thought to lead to murder, were believed to consign the soul to hell. The first and worst was considered to be pride, because it was Satan's sin and brought into being all the rest.

Justice is the prerogative of man over man, in a hierarchical society, but it should be tempered with mercy, which 'droppeth as the gentle rain from heaven' (*The Merchant of Venice*). This divine attribute, shown by God in his judgement of Adam and Eve (when he commuted the death sentence and let his son take away the sins of mankind) is referred to and demonstrated in many plays, such as *The Tempest*. Justice without mercy is seen as tyrannical and inhumane, as shown in *Measure for Measure*. Justice is cognate with 'judgement', another keyword and concept in many Elizabethan plays.

Machiavelli's self-help philosophy concerning the necessity for the ruthless eradication of enemies was the inspiration for the behaviour of many a Shakespeare villain, e.g. Claudius, Iago and Edmund. Looking after your own interests is presented by the amoral Machiavels as the only logical and effective way to proceed in life. The end justifies the means, and guilt and repentance are for fools and weaklings. This philosophy clashed completely with medieval fatalism and the Christian precepts of loving thy neighbour and the Ten Commandments, thus questioning the fundamental tenets of Elizabethan morality.

Women were possessions, financially dependent on men to whom they owed love, honour and obedience — and domestic labour — first as daughters and then as wives. Divided loyalties could be caused, as in the cases of Desdemona and Cordelia, by conflicting demands of father and husband. This could have serious consequences for the woman in question, who risked being disowned and deprived of a home and place in society. Servant women, usually widowed or unmarried, had to please their masters or find themselves out on the streets, which is why Juliet's nurse is forced to side against her. Mothers such as Juliet's and Hamlet's also have to put their husbands' wishes above their children's needs (a priority still in evidence in Dickens, e.g. Mrs Gradgrind in *Hard Times*) because of their precarious social position and fear of being abandoned for failing in their wifely duties. Sometimes women disobey a husband to help a son, since he could become a replacement breadwinner and source of financial support, but they cannot take risks for a daughter. Women could rise only through their association with high-ranking men, hence Lady Macbeth's desire to see her husband crowned. Old men could purchase pretty young wives, who were sometimes able to get their revenge, as in Chaucer's tales of the Miller and the Merchant.

The idea of the fickle female was a classical literary stereotype fostered by the medieval Church, whose own misogyny was founded on the premise that untrustworthy Eve betrayed her husband and all mankind when she allowed herself to be seduced by a smooth-talking serpent. Fortune was often represented by a woman with a wheel that she turned at random; the inconstant moon is always referred to as female in literature of the medieval and Elizabethan periods, and later. Chaucer and Shakespeare wrote about the faithless Criseyde/Cressida, and Hamlet rails against the frailty of women.

Students might wonder at the insistence on female chastity in so many of their pre-1900 set texts. The security of society and peace of mind of men are dependent upon women's virginity before marriage — making them a bargaining tool for advantageous marriages to benefit a father's social status and extended family — and faithfulness after it. For this reason, young women were chaperoned to avoid ever finding themselves alone with a man. Being cuckolded — made a hornèd beast — and laughed at was the worst fear of men at the time. In a society that passed inheritance down the male line through primogeniture, it was necessary to be certain that your heir was indeed your son and not someone else's bastard, for illegitimacy was a threat to family harmony and the wider social fabric (see *King Lear*). Virginity and chastity were linked to religion via the Virgin Mary and were regarded not only as an ideal state for women but also as a test of the nobility of men, since only the higher orders were thought able to resist the temptations of the flesh (hence Prospero's strictures on the subject to Ferdinand in *The Tempest*). Close same-sex friendships and avowals of love, however, must not be automatically assumed to carry sexual overtones, since there were classical and Biblical ideals of non-physical bonds of affection between men.

Humorous writing

It may be that one or more of the plays or novels you are studying for examination or coursework belongs to the genre of humorous writing, either primarily or as a secondary element, as with a Shakespeare comedy or a Jane Austen novel, for instance. It is therefore necessary to know something about how humour is created, so that you can identify and discuss in detail the text's use of techniques of plot, characterisation and language to achieve amusing effects, and to enable you to differentiate between the different types of humour present. This knowledge is also necessary for approaching unseen texts for criticism.

Humour generally falls into one of four categories: the inappropriate, the misunderstood, the unexpected and the undesired. The following tables convey the hierarchical nature of comic devices, with verbal dexterity being considered the highest-order skill and visual humour the lowest, and the devices are rank-ordered within each section. Literary works tend to aim for the top end of the scale, whereas light entertainment draws on the middle and lower sections. Some literary texts, however — such as the plays of Tom Stoppard — make use of the full range of available devices.

Verbal

Device/genre	Example
Wit	Puns/repartee
Irony	Saying opposite of truth
Satire	Sarcasm
Parody	Exaggerating tone
Neologism	Nonsense language
Misuse	Malapropism
Trivialising	Litotes (understatement)
Aggrandising	Hyperbole (overstatement)
Bawdy	Double entendre
Euphemism	Avoiding embarrassing word
Caricature	Catch phrase
Dialect	Unknown vocabulary
Accent	Upper-class drawl
Naming	Matches character
After-dinner speaking	Telling long anecdote
Stand-up comedy	Telling short joke
Double act	Stupid stooge
Scatological	Mention of lavatories

Situational

Device/genre	Example
Irony	Unexpected twist
Sketch	Mocking a situation
Black humour	Showing disrespect
Absurd humour	Reversing roles
Stereotyping	Predictable attitude
Deception	Substituted object
Disguise	Mistaken identity

Visual

Device/genre	Example
Silent comedy	Cliff-hanger
Mime	Exaggerated body language
Pantomime	Cross-dressing
Bedroom farce	Timing of entrance
Slapstick	Custard pie
Clowning	Falling over an obstacle
Cartoons	Inflicting violence
Puppets	Grotesque appearance

There are techniques guaranteed to evoke laughter, though they are not necessarily to the credit of the human race! If anyone is made to look ridiculous, say something silly, do something embarrassing, the audience will be amused; comedy is about breaking the rules and deviating from the norm. A text may predominantly rely on puns, ambiguous language, double entendre and witty adaptation of famous quotations; or on bizarre appearance, caricatures, clowning, catch phrases and silly names, such as 'M'Choakumchild'; or the middle range of situational humour, which clashes class, race, gender or generations (the formula of all television situation comedies) in order to create confusion and a predicament. The many comic devices that can be identified in daily use in the full range of media are also employed in literary texts.

Approaches to literary texts

LITERATURE

Studying English Literature

Framework for reading

Without a framework of reference and an understanding of how poetry, prose or plays work, the reader will be unable to respond meaningfully or have the critical vocabulary with which to express that response. Literature students have to learn to read more widely and deeply than the casual reader, to register all the elements that make up text. They need to understand not only what they read but also how they read through a process of active interpretation based on informed judgement. Below are aspects of text that you should notice when reading.

Plot, character and dialogue

Do you want to read on? How have you been made to want to find out what happens? Do you care about the characters? How have you been made to identify with them? Curiosity is an acknowledged factor in the reading process, but curiosity has to be stimulated and the literature student examines how this has been achieved. Plots can cover a few hours or hundreds of years and concern one main character or generations of them. Characterisation is achieved by a variety of means that need observing, including speech habits, clothing or objects associated with characters, frequency of appearance in the work and in which combinations, as well as the obvious means of portrayal through physical traits, personality and behaviour. Who gets to do the talking, to whom and about what? How often is dialogue used and what is its contribution to the work? (Jane Austen's novels are over 90% dialogue, which is what makes them easy to dramatise.)

Setting, atmosphere and mood

These are closely related but distinguishable elements of text that non-literature students may not consciously observe, though they would notice if they did not conform to expectation for the genre (e.g. if a ghost story were set on a sunny day on a beach or if an elegy contained cheerful images). Casual readers complain if the progression of a narrative is held up by description in a novel, whereas literary readers need to be aware of the function and effect of choice of place, time of day, season, weather, colours and decors, and the adjectives that go with them.

Theme, imagery and diction

Readers need to be alert to the recurrences of words, objects, places and ideas that give a text its integrity, pattern and meaning. (For instance, the word 'judgement' and its relatives are used 116 times in *Mansfield Park*; Keats uses the adjective 'sweet' in 54 poems.) Noticing these repetitions and asking yourself why they exist gives you direct access to the heart of a text. Certain words and images carry immediate significance because of their traditional associations derived from their use in religion and mythology, such as dark for evil, fire for punishment, fruit for temptation, falling for death. Vocabulary choices create a sense of historical period and social context, as well as affecting characterisation and narrative voice.

Structure, style and register

A literary text has been arranged in a certain order, and the reader has to ask why this order and not another, and what effect juxtaposition, time-jumps, flashbacks or recurrence are creating. Like a piece of music or an artistic composition, a literary text must harmoniously relate its parts to its whole, and sections or chapter divisions or verse breaks are there for a purpose.

Register consists of the generic choices of colloquial or formal, spoken or written, simple or complex, archaic or contemporary language. In addition, particular grammatical or literary devices constitute style, which is more than a vehicle for content; the two are mutually reinforcing and forge meaning together in poetry and prose. Writers can be recognised by their style, which is as individual as a fingerprint.

Filling in the gaps

Intelligent reading of narrative involves the reader in filling in the gaps, which can be proved by asking someone to turn a sequence of photos or a string of individual words into a narrative. If readers are presented with apparently unconnected paragraphs or lines of poetry, they will nonetheless try to make connections and create meaning from them, which demonstrates the active role played in the decoding of text and construction of meaning. The important thing is that the reader should be aware of where the gaps are and why, what determined the way in which they filled them, and what this tells us about ways of interpreting text.

Realising the choices

All texts are fictional to some degree, because they all select, organise and prioritise material from a certain perspective — even television news bulletins — and every included word, character, event or piece of information imply others that were rejected as not suitable or desirable for some reason. All presence denotes absence, and the reader needs constantly to ask why something is there (it will not be accidental) and what was excluded. Any story is just one among a potentially infinite number of versions that might be told. Likewise all oppositions privilege one side or the other, and in fiction this is achieved by loading viewpoint and voice so that the reader is led to identify with one side and share its assumptions. Use of a particular setting or landscape can also manipulate the weighting of sympathy; for instance, as a rule we are on the side of country dwellers rather than urbanites. However, this is the legacy of Romanticism and would not necessarily have been true before 1775 — when nature was considered wild, threatening and uncivilised — so we must be constantly alert to changes in cultural and historical influences.

Recognising the codes

Just as it is a convention that films have full-orchestra soundtrack music (even in the middle of the desert), that characters in musicals burst into a synchronised song-and-dance routine at the drop of a hat, that German soldiers helpfully speak English in war films, there are codes governing the creation of narrative fiction and drama (in which, for instance, characters talk to themselves). These conventions are absurd when one stops to think about them, but we usually do not, hence the concept of the 'willing suspension of disbelief'. Like other discourses, literature has embedded codes, conscious or unconscious signposts to position readers and lead them down a predetermined trail as far as possible, through the use of associative expectations. As Fay Weldon has pointed out, all writers start out as readers, so the expectations and codes are automatically perpetuated. These conventions of genre and form set up such familiarisation that we are not even aware of being manipulated as readers. To call the reader's attention to something, or create irony or humour, it is necessary to defamiliarise, by suddenly using an incongruous word, or anachronism (like Red Riding Hood having a gun in her knickers in the Roald Dahl version of the fairy tale), or breaking out of the restriction of form, or reversing the stereotype (Don Quixote, the unheroic knight, did that as early as 1605), or pushing the convention to the extreme, such as starting the life of the main character from conception rather than from birth. Such breaking of codes means that new mixed or anti-genres can develop as models for other code-breakers: the modern fairy tale, promoted by Angela Carter among others, is now a genre in its own right.

In literature, as in politics, everything either supports or reacts against the status quo. Real reading is one of the most social and political activities humans can engage in, which is why both totalitarian and democratic governments see it as a tool of control for conservation or change. For this reason we should constantly question and uncover what we take for granted and thereby develop a heightened responsiveness and autonomy; as Montaigne warned, 'we need to interpret interpretations'.

Annotating text

Most schools expect students to buy their own copies of the texts that will be studied during the course. Some provide copies of texts free of charge to students on condition that they return them unannotated. This is understandable economically, but students' exam performance reflects their 'ownership' of and engagement with the text, and their ability to prepare it appropriately and find their way around it quickly in exam conditions. You may be tempted to use a copy already annotated by someone else, but there is no substitute for the learning involved in making your own marginal comments and underlinings. In any case, students often want to keep their copies of set texts as a start to their personal libraries, especially if they particularly enjoyed them or are going on to read English at university.

Why annotate?

Although the boards vary, it is likely that the majority of your exams will be open-book tests and you would therefore be at a disadvantage not to have a text annotated to the same degree as other students. The return of the closed-book exam (to allay fears of cheating through excessive annotation) is unfortunate because it is unnatural to be asked to comment at length on something you do not have access to. However, it is just as important, if not more so, to annotate closed texts, as it benefits not only the learning but the selection and recall processes too. Coursework texts also need to provide a source of notes and quotations, and you will find it easier to gather material if you have annotated your text judiciously on first reading and again after discovering the coursework title. If you need to retake an exam module or resubmit coursework, with or without further tuition, it would aid you considerably to have an annotated text to return to. An ability to annotate a text fully, but not excessively, is a skill that will serve you well for the unseen criticism module of A2 as well as for each set text, and is one that needs practice from KS3 onwards.

The guidelines for permissible annotation are that it must be brief and marginal, within and adjacent to the body of the text, excluding end papers and blank pages between chapters. Extraneous pieces of paper and adhesive labels are not permitted, but there does not appear to be a restriction on the turning down of page corners to help you find significant passages more easily. Annotation is allowed for the purpose of glossing, cross-referencing and highlighting useful quotations, but not to aid essay planning. As exact essay titles cannot be predicted and standard plans will not earn high marks (because they lack focus on the question), it is not in any case in your interests to plan essays in the text. It is likely that in the future A-level will become a clean-text exam, as has already been decreed for GCSE English Literature — as a compromise between open- and closed-book exams. This will still make it desirable to have become familiar with an annotated text before you are issued with your virgin copy as you go into the exam.

How to annotate?

It is a good idea to use pencil for all book annotations because you can then change your mind without making the text difficult to read. If you are reusing for the comparative synoptic unit a text you studied with different objectives for an earlier module, adding and removing notes in the margin and underlined quotations may be necessary to refocus on the new topic.

The most frequent mistake students make is to highlight or underline huge chunks of text so that there is no longer any way of distinguishing key points and phrases. In extreme cases, students have more text highlighted than not, which renders the annotation process useless. Examiners advise students to incorporate into their exam and coursework essays short, integrated quotations and to avoid long ones (which are time-consuming, contain much that is redundant and indicate that you are a student who has difficulty in identifying essential ideas). On a typical page, you should expect to have only one or two underlinings and marginal notes — probably keywords relating to themes. One examiner comments that 'fewer prepared notes in texts would help to generate a fresher and more relevant approach', particularly to Shakespeare questions. This would also avoid 'sameness of essays within some centres' and 'what are clearly unassimilated notes'. The fact that your teacher says something in class about a text does not make it automatically necessary or desirable for you to write it in your book.

However, another mistake students make is to think that it does not matter, as long as the majority of the text is annotated, if there are whole chapters, scenes or poems that are unmarked. You are tempting fate to believe that your blank pages will not be the ones set for a passage-based or poetry question in the exam.

What to annotate?

When you first read through a new exam text on your own, there are things you will probably wish to note that refer to general themes, character, plot and comparisons with other texts. At this stage there may be some question marks or exclamation marks in the margins (which can be removed later if they are in pencil). During the next stage, as you study the text in detail in class, your teacher will point out important ideas and quotations for you to underline. Margin comments need to be kept very brief — usually no more than two or three words, and often a single word will suffice. The aim is not to explain what is happening on the page, for you will know this perfectly well by the time you sit the exam, but to remind yourself of the significance of an aspect of the content or language, in relation to the overall themes or style of the work. Such short phrases are quickly seen and understood if you need to scan your text for essay-planning material. As there is no restriction on the use of different coloured pens or highlighters, you could adopt a system of coded colours to distinguish, for instance, character points from imagery points.

Where a specified edition includes a foreword or set of notes at the back, students are expected to make use of 'editorial material or textual commentary published in the editions studied', so these parts of the text also need study and relevant annotation, and the student who does not take them into account will be at a disadvantage. It is not unknown for examiners to quote a sentence from an introduction as an essay question. Bear in mind, however, that since the examiners will recognise immediately any material you include in your essay that comes from a source you have with you in the exam, they will not be impressed by lengthy quotations from it.

Consulting critics

Assessment Objective 4 requires candidates to 'articulate independent opinions and judgements, informed by different interpretations of literary texts by other readers', and essay titles often quote a critical comment. The exam boards suggest that 'contrasting the views of early critics and reviewers...with those of later commentators is a rewarding way to explore the idea of plurality' (OCR 2000 Teacher Support). Note that while you should collect the views of others on the text you are studying, the objective contains the keyword 'independent'. By all means take into account the views of editors and critics, teachers and peers, but be discerning and selective, make sure they are relevant and supportable, and integrate them into your interpretation of a text rather than adopt them as a substitute for your own views. To quote from examiners' comments, to achieve a grade A candidates are required to 'show a freshness of personal response as opposed to mere repetitions of someone else's critical opinions, however good'. Your teachers will probably advise you not to consult critics until you have become familiar enough with a text to form your own opinions of it, and to be discerning in your choice of critical sources.

The meaning of a literary work may be debatable, not because of author incompetence but because of a recognition of the ambiguities and complexities of existence. *Hamlet*, for instance, has no definitive interpretation and, on the contrary, invites mutually exclusive ones. Literary critics not only often disagree fundamentally with each other on matters of literary interpretation, but sometimes they disagree with themselves and over a period of years retract a previous view confidently offered to the public. (The famous Cambridge literary critic F. R. Leavis originally considered the great tradition of English fiction writers to consist of Austen, Eliot, James, Conrad and Lawrence; his omission of Dickens was later remedied after a change of heart.)

Student magazines

There are two quarterly English A-level magazines: *The English Review* for A-level English Literature and *emagazine* for both Language and Literature students. They are different in style and cover different aspects of syllabus options, so both are recommended. The magazines liaise with schools and publish articles on specific authors, set texts and critical theory. They are written in academic but accessible language and format by lecturers, teachers, examiners and well-known contemporary writers. They contain stimulating ideas, practical support and time-saving research. What they offer you between them are fresh approaches and new ideas for syllabus texts, suggestions for wider reading, academic essay models, the views of other readers, unseen criticism practice, advice on skills, sample student essays, specialist knowledge, up-to-date exam information, teacher/examiner insights and familiarity with the use of literary terminology. Schools can acquire any number of half-price subscriptions for their staff and students provided that the school library pays for one full-price subscription.

Study guides

Most commercial guides are aimed at average to weaker students and some have misleadingly oversimplified summaries and superficial interpretations. The confidence and competence they claim to offer can be illusory, as the only means of genuinely acquiring these skills is through engagement and familiarity with the actual text. Guides by definition are a repository of second-hand opinions, which may restrict your ability to form more independent and sophisticated ones. Examiners are looking for first-hand knowledge, demonstrable understanding of text and a convincingly personal response, none of which is possible for a student who has relied on a secondary source. Examiners also recognise the unassimilated concepts, lack of evidence, incoherent argument, missing focus, stale approach and inconsistent expression of the student who has lifted too much from a study guide — as well as the actual phrases and ideas, which they get to know only too well. There are, however, some publications that offer excellent critical approaches to texts, but you need to know which they are and to use them as a supplement to, and not a mainstay of, your own response to a text.

Biographies

Students are often tempted to access biographical information about their set-text authors. This can contribute to an understanding of historical and social background, but you need to handle such information carefully in your essays, as it is not likely to be relevant to answering the question and is, strictly speaking, not relevant to the study of literature. Knowing biographical detail can prejudice your response to a writer and work, so unless you find evidence within the text that it is relevant, you should not let biographical knowledge influence your interpretation. With a few exceptions (such as Sylvia Plath, whose poems are so personal as to be virtually unintelligible otherwise), it is not necessary to know anything about authors other than the period in which they wrote, their gender, class, race, geographical location and, perhaps, religious or political beliefs. These add up to what is called the extratextual context, which gives us pointers to the aims and themes of the work. It is useful to know what specialised words or coinages meant to writers who constructed a philosophy around them, such as 'mendacity' in Tennessee Williams, Hardy's 'nescience' and Keats's 'negative capability', but again this intratextual knowledge must be supported by, not imposed on, the text.

The internet

It can be tempting to turn to the internet when you are stuck with an essay, in a panic about exam revision or just want to know something about a new text or author.

However, you must be wary: internet material — over 90% of which is American — is frequently ungrammatical, repetitive and unstructured, and can be a bad style model for literature essay writing. The material will probably not focus on your particular essay title, may be factually erroneous, and there is no guarantee that it is of A-level standard. If it were publishable in book form or academically respectable, it would probably not be available for free on the internet. Some websites, however, are a convenient and time-saving research tool, and are especially useful for checking titles and dates, for finding quotations, and for counting the usage of particular words or phrases in a text.

Conferences and festivals

Sixth-form conferences and Easter revision courses are growing in availability and popularity. They are run by publishers or consultancy organisations that, although profit-making, have educational aims and hire critics, authors, university lecturers and chief examiners as speakers or presenters. They have many advantages: they are tailored to your own exam board; you get to meet and share views with peers studying the same texts in other schools; they offer new perspectives and quotable material; examiners give first-hand advice from experience; revision is given a timely focus and incentive; study materials are on offer which you may not know about or which are not available in shops.

In addition, more than 30 literary festivals are held all over the UK each year. These provide unique opportunities to hear authors and critics talk about texts you may be studying, and to follow debates on wider aspects of literary studies.

Critical works

These include the introductions to the specified editions of your texts, which will mean more to you if you look at them after rather than before reading the texts for the first time. Your teacher may in addition provide you with other articles and critical extracts. Whole works of criticism tend to be aimed at university level and many are too dense, remote, detailed or whimsical to be of obvious relevance or help at A-level. It is particularly necessary to have recommendations for Shakespeare criticism, as there is a bewildering amount available, some of it now old-fashioned and discredited. Used as a basis for class discussion, and followed up in writing, critical comments that are properly explored, evaluated and assimilated into your own view of a text can be usefully supportive of your interpretation.

There are two series of collected criticism that can be recommended for their coverage of major themes and their appropriateness for A-level studies: *A Collection of Critical Essays* (previously known as *Twentieth Century Views*) published by Prentice-Hall, which is author-based, and the Macmillan Case Books, which focus on individual works. The former reproduces critical essays in their entirety, while the latter consists of a historical compilation of extracts from the works of

famous critics, which contribute to an understanding of cultural contexts and influences to fulfil AO5.

Reading for bias

What a text denotes and what it connotes are different. Literature serves the interests of certain groups in society and is a reflection of the values of the society in which it was written. Encoded assumptions can be traced back to a socioeconomic basis and political ideology which controls literature and therefore controls people's choices and behaviours. Terry Eagleton urges us to read against the grain to see the oppression and prejudice behind the text, by which he means bias of gender, class and race. According to Wendy Morgan:

■ Any text is made in a particular society at a particular time. This influences the form it takes and the ideas it represents.

■ Any text gives you a particular version (or part) of a story; it emphasises certain things, and it has gaps and is silent about things.

■ Texts don't contain one fixed, definite meaning put there by the author. Different kinds of readers in different societies and times can produce different meanings for the same text because of what they bring to it.

■ Any text offers you a way of seeing and valuing things and invites you to accept its version of the truth, the way things are meant to be. What comes to be accepted as the truth, as knowledge, comes to serve someone's interests.

(*Critical Literacy in the Classroom*, Routledge, 1997)

Exclusion

There are various kinds of bias; the most pervasive and distorting, but also the most difficult to detect, is complete exclusion, as in the case of, for instance, non-heterosexual relationships for many centuries, although so many writers were and are homosexual — not to mention a significant percentage of the population. Jane Austen notoriously did not mention the servants, without whom the members of the leisured gentry class depicted in her genteel novels could not run their large houses and families. Because, therefore, readers cannot identify with or mirror that which is absent, they are forced to accept what is on offer as the norm and to try to see themselves as part of it. William Golding, a boys' prep-school teacher, admitted that he did not include girls in *Lord of the Flies* because it would have complicated matters. Hence generations of schoolchildren study a novel that denies not only the relevance but even the existence of half of the human race, inevitably sending the message that the male experience is the one that counts. This is in addition to the ubiquitous use of the non-inclusive 'he', which can, allegedly, stand for both genders. (The fallacy of this claim can be proved by the usual response to the suggestion that 'he' should be replaced by 'she' as the universal pronoun.)

If we consider the family and friend relationships traditionally presented in literary texts (Shakespeare provides many examples), it soon becomes apparent which ones are noticeable by their absence. These are (or were at least until recently) relationships between sisters, mothers and daughters, female friendships, female gangs — i.e. any all-female relationship. Jane Austen's novels contain women but do not explore the private world of women and what they think and feel about each other. Even now, when homosexual relationships are portrayed in fiction, they are rarely lesbian (the marked form with its own name).

Marginalisation

Women see differently from men, but because there have been few women in the traditional literary canon (only 5 out of 150 appear in *The Penguin Book of English Verse*), and because the vast majority of main characters and narrators have been male, the female view has always been marginalised. There have been a few (shocking in their time) celebrated cases of male authors adopting female protagonists — in *Anna Karenina*, *Tess of the D'Urbervilles*, *Clarissa*, *Madame Bovary* — but they are women portrayed as men see them (attractive, sensual and sexually desirable) and who are then convicted by society and 'executed' for being so. From Chaucer onwards, women in literature have been defined in relation to men, i.e. as maids (virgins), wives, widows, mistresses or whores. Until recently there were no other categories for women, either professional or personal, and therefore swapping one category for another is their only possible movement, and not one that is self-determined. There are no male equivalents for most of these socioeconomic states, and in any case fiction allows men to be more than just husbands or widowers, their marital status being of secondary importance to their real function in life. As Robert Graves said, 'Men do, women are', and Byron claimed, 'Man's love is to man's life a thing apart/'Tis women's whole existence.'

Because most authors in English have been middle-class and white, the same marginalisation process has occurred with class and race. This has created the judgemental concepts of 'the Norm' and 'the Other', with the latter being relegated to the ghetto. Unless girls pretend to be boys and adopt boys' names in certain famous children's stories, they cannot be accepted in the gang and be eligible for adventures. This is a paradigm for their portrayal in texts when older too. Naming (and taming) is a major factor in the division between the Norm and the Other (e.g. Owen having his name changed to Roland in Friel's *Translations*), and it has been man's prerogative since Adam in the Garden of Eden to do the naming.

One of the effects of the literary marginalisation of women is that their mythologies and hero figures have not become part of the mainstream. We hear a lot about Eve's failings and submission, but little about her predecessor Lilith (Adam's first wife according to Jewish mythology), who rebelled against the injustice of her not having been created equal. Women's biological experiences of childbirth, rape and menstruation have been considered taboo because they are irrelevant or embarrassing to men. There are plenty of literary examples, however, of examinations of the male libido and its appendages and functions. Feminist writing stresses the importance of the female body as a source of legitimate literary imagery, to win it back from its prevalent use as the language of pornography and swearing, in which the worst terms of abuse are words for female genitalia or violent sexual penetration.

Viewpoint

The narrative voice, whether male or female, is the next step in constructing bias in a literary work. If it is unspecified, the voice is assumed to be male, as in the KS2/3 reader *The Turbulent Term of Tyke Tyler* and the first part of *To Kill a Mockingbird* — and note the gendered words 'Tyke' and 'Scout'. We are not just allowed to see only certain things, but we are directed to see them through the evaluating eyes of the narrator; whoever reveals the situation controls the response to it. Some male authors have had the confidence to assume that they can understand the female mind to the extent of adopting a female narrator, starting with Daniel Defoe's *Moll Flanders* in 1722 (though it is hard to find examples of the reverse). So it is well established that men do the seeing (subjects) and women are the seen (objects). It is always worth bearing in mind that a Marxist or feminist perspective would see things very differently; and it would be a different story even if told from the point of view of another character. Wordsworth felt strongly that peasants, women and children deserved a mention and a viewpoint in poetry, and he adopted their perspective in his own work, though this was a radical practice at the time.

Often the basis of fiction is the battle between good and evil, overtly portrayed or represented by another binary opposition (such as facts versus fantasy in *Hard Times*), and the reader is positioned by authorial or narrative voice and viewpoint to know which side to be on — through having to identify with, to mirror, the attractive characters and to condemn what the narrator/author condemns.

Being framed

Some literary works in verse and prose have a fictional or nonfictional prologue and/or epilogue (e.g. Tennyson's 'Morte d'Arthur' and *The Taming of the Shrew*) or a parallel story (e.g. *The Canterbury Tales*), which act as a framing device. The existence of a frame not only adds depth, variety and another dimension, often ironic, but it also influences reader response through the juxtaposition of characters, narratives and settings on the different levels. The old Leo who tells the story of the downfall of the young Leo in *The Go-Between* has already prepared the reader to be suspicious of all the adult characters about to be introduced. In *The Canterbury Tales,* for instance, the character with the highest social status, the Knight, tells his tale first so that the lower-class pilgrims, particularly the Miller, can be judged harshly by comparison.

Taken for granted

Another form of bias is assumption — how readers' expectations determine their interpretations. If a news report tells us that a young woman wearing a short skirt was raped while walking home alone at night, the likely dominant reading would be that she was to blame. This is an example of a cautionary tale that constructs gender, the overall implication being that it is the woman's fault rather than the unknown attacker's, and that the victim can therefore justifiably expect to suffer more than the victimiser. The social consequences of such ingrained attitudes — upheld by judges — are the curtailing of women's freedoms of dress and movement and the implicit acceptability of violent crimes against women.

We do not usually question these assumptions, which are by definition uncon-scious and therefore difficult to eradicate, and so they continue to reinforce cultural attitudes every time they are activated. They have the status of known facts, though they are really only privileged interpretations that operate in the interests of some community groups and against the interests of others, in this case pro-men and anti-women. Another long-held assumption propagated in texts well into the twentieth century was that girls, colonial nations and the working classes did not need, or should not receive, education.

The same dominant readings govern literary interpretation in all genres and at all levels. Even the comic children's poem 'Jabberwocky' has an easily discernible gendered narrative code: it tells of a heroic deed by a lone young male against a terrifying monster; it is a rite of passage to impress his father (the participants are all male because the poem is in the adventure genre). The winner of a recent national competition for the most popular poem of all time was Rudyard Kipling's 'If', which ends with '…you'll be a man, my son' and makes a multitude of questionable assumptions about the role of public schools, colonial administrators and masculinity. Once again, females are invisible.

What's in a word?

Words conjure memories and emotions, good or bad: there are very few, if any, completely neutral words, since everyday and apparently innocuous words such as 'cake' or 'knife' and 'home' or 'hospital' have connotations attached to them. Advertisers, for instance, know and capitalise on this. The most commonly used adjectives for character description — 'beautiful', 'blue-eyed' and 'blonde' — are also laden with aesthetic and moral values and are prejudiced against those who are 'other'. Even synonyms can have different values, so that 'slim' is desirable, but 'skinny' or 'thin' is not (though the difference in size is probably not quantifiable). Certain words, such as 'dead', are avoided altogether or replaced by euphemisms to avoid negative responses. Right is privileged over left, going back to classical augury, when sinister (meaning 'on the left') omens meant impending catastrophe, thus discriminating against left-handers.

Although the marked forms 'poetess' and 'authoress' are rejected by female writers as being quaint and patronising, 'poet', 'playwright' and 'author' are assumed to be male unless otherwise stated, as are 'surgeon' and 'professor'. The term 'female author' signifies gender, but this is again a marked form and a deviation from the norm. This no-win situation also affects race, as 'black youth' appears to be stressing colour and arousing prejudice, but unqualified 'youth' implies white. There are some derogatory verbs and adjectives that are specifically associated with women or that have no male equivalent — 'nag', 'gossip', 'flirt', 'hysterical', 'bitchy' — and a whole phalanx of words to disapprove of sexually active females from the Elizabethan alehouse to the present-day school playground — 'trollop', 'whore', 'drab', 'bawd', 'punk', 'callet', 'strumpet', 'crumpet', 'tart', 'slut' and 'slapper'. ('Playboy', 'stud' and 'hunk' do not carry any critical overtone, rather the reverse.)

Gender pairs much used in literature, such as governor/governess, landlord/landlady, master/mistress, are not in fact socially or morally equal, with the male form being the privileged half of the pair, just as the active and fun things in popular culture have always been male-specific: cowboy, boy scout, Superman, Walkman, Game Boy. (The *Little Miss* children's books were as much of a second-rate afterthought to the hugely successful *Mr Men* series as Eve was to Adam.) Feminists go further and claim that language is a male construct designed for male use in a public arena and that it therefore cannot represent female viewpoints and needs. As Bathsheba says in *Far From the Madding Crowd*, 'It is difficult for a woman to define her feelings in language which is chiefly made by men to express theirs.'

Constructing difference

'The difference of view' (Virginia Woolf's phrase) is a social construction rather than a biological one. In gender terms, femininity is constructed as timid, weak, passive, static, dependent and unambitious. This is because masculinity claims the dominant, active and privileged half of all the binary oppositions that underlie reading and writing practices and social roles (science/art; talking/listening; war/peace). Acceptance in society and confidence in identity depend on conforming to these differences, and there are penalties for characters who show the attributes allocated to the other gender (e.g. Antony must die for being drawn into femininity by Cleopatra). These constructions go back to ancient civilisations engaged in combat, when warmongers needed to be balanced by homemakers for the survival of society, and life was divided into the public and the private spheres. Gender, like race, is cultural not biological; not all males are physically strong and brave and athletic, but they are socially engineered to believe that these characteristics are necessary attributes of masculinity.

Embodiment is the crossroads between biology/sex and sociology/gender. The visual and literary arts have programmed women to be on show for the purpose of attracting admiration for their physical features with no regard for their mental qualities, constructing women's identity as only a body. However, bodies age and decay; ageing women in life and in literature are not considered attractive, whereas greying Rochesters abound in fiction and television newsrooms. It could be argued that this sense of built-in obsolescence focuses women's attention towards their own bodies and the need to strive for physical perfection, men's admiration and other women's envy, thus leaving them with little time for or interest in serious decision making, especially as they are also occupied by home-running and child-raising. This reinforces both the control that patriarchal codes have over society and also women's own views of their socioeconomic role.

A major area of constructed gender difference in all but very recent literature lies in the common beliefs that women do not enjoy sex, cannot have proper orgasms, are naturally monogamous and want to have lots of children. Traditionally, any woman who dares to disagree with these beliefs reveals herself not to be a proper woman and is vilified by society. Freud, by asking, 'What does woman want?' (a question still asked today but at least as old as the Middle Ages and featured in Chaucer's 'The Wife of Bath's Tale') gave psychoanalytical reinforcement to the construct of women as a mysterious and therefore unequal Other (no one has ever asked, 'What does man want?') This has caused women to be viewed as unfathomable and irrational, and therefore the object of fear and ostracism (and accusations of witchcraft at worst, and of possessing female intuition at best).

Girls are gendered to see things from a male point of view as well as a female one, whereas boys are gendered to avoid anything 'girly' and to dismiss their mothers in adolescence as a rite of passage. It is a fact that boys complain in a mixed or single-sex class about having to study *Emma* or *Jane Eyre*, while girls do not complain about doing *Lord of the Flies* or a predominantly male Shakespeare text. Girls, too, would rather identify with a strong male character than with a subordinate and marginalised female one, and so they are used to switching gender perspective. Bestselling children's books are as much male-oriented as ever; a character called Harriet Potter would not have made her creator so rich.

Stereotyping

Stereotypes are basic elements of all discourse and have become such universal literary signifiers that you may not be aware that you expect someone hunchbacked to be evil, or someone large and rosy-cheeked to be cheerful, or someone with a long, white beard to be wise and trustworthy. However, authors exploit these stereotypes to determine reader response, or subvert them with the consequence that the anti-stereotype becomes an alternative stereotype. Though stereotypes may reflect life as we know it, they also ensure the perpetuation of it, and the limited range of role models and behaviour patterns on offer to certain groups of readers. Were all women for many centuries really content to be housebound housekeepers with a bunch of keys? Were there really hordes of happy, starving poor and cheerfully faithful feudal retainers in Victorian Britain? Were all colonised natives sexual predators, the devil's spawn and would-be murderers as suggested in *The Tempest*?

In colonial discourse, the stereotype used to be the benevolent invader with superior knowledge and good intentions, who was always under threat from the ungrateful, would-be rebellious natives. In reaction against Ballantyne's 'Boys' Own'-style adventure novel *Coral Island*, in *Lord of the Flies* Golding unmasked the stereotypes of the white civilised man versus the cannibals (Calibans) and portrayed choirboys as the real barbarians. Brian Friel's *Translations* also calls into question the concept of an inferior, savage, subjected race in need of enlightenment by showing the chief 'colonist' to be an insensitive, ill-educated, bullying tyrant. The literature of the colonisers played a substantial role in the process of colonisation, and generations of schoolchildren in the empire on which the sun never set had to chant Wordsworth's 'Daffodils', although they had never seen a daffodil and probably never would.

Racial or class stereotypes are prevalent in literary works of all periods, from the comic 'rude mechanicals' of *A Midsummer Night's Dream* to Sam, the working-class hobbit and devoted servant who calls his peer and master 'Mr' Frodo. Jews have appeared consistently as being obsessed with money, and female servants are always willing to provide other services for their aristocratic employers. This, of course, like all stereotypes, reflects a social reality of a particular period that is then perpetuated by reinforcement in works of literature.

Think about the story of Little Red Riding Hood and the stereotypical roles involved: redundant, widowed, bedridden granny; domestic mother who bakes and is responsible for granny; vulnerable, naive, gullible daughter who disobeys and is not safe outside the house; male wolf who kills helpless, elderly woman in order to prey on appetising little girl; strong man with an axe who comes to the rescue and heroically slays his opponent, thereby saving daughter and granny (who is cut out of the dead wolf by the woodcutter/father figure).

Similar stereotypes exist in all literary genres. Examine the cultural codes of race and gender underlying Westerns, for instance, and you will find that:

- men are powerful and have jobs, possess horses (which are subject to commands, are a means of transport, give height and therefore dominance); men have weapons and use them impressively

- women are largely absent, stay indoors, do not move or get to speak; women provide services (drink, sex, schoolteaching, homemaking)
- 'Red Indians' and outlaws are dark-haired and dark-skinned, and live in the wilderness
- good (dressed in white, or with a white horse) always wins; law is not enforced in a courtroom, but in a medieval duel between a good man and a bad man

Punishing the rebels

Starting with biblical bad women and on through medieval folklore, women who step out of line or are disobedient are punished for it, like Little Red Riding Hood. Unconventional women, like native rebels, either learn to conform or die. They die of a broken heart, as victims of their own longings, or commit suicide while of unsound mind. The list is endless, but includes Ophelia, Bertha Mason, Miss Havisham, the Lady of Shalott, Eustacia Vye, Lady Macbeth, Cathy Linton, Madame Bovary and Anna Karenina. Men cannot be allowed to commit suicide — as it is deemed a weak and cowardly act — so must be killed by illness or by another man, hence the attraction of duels at dawn long after they became illegal. Men also have the option of joining the army to get themselves killed, often achieving heroic status and the gratitude of their country at the same time.

Narrative is a means of resolving philosophical dilemmas and containing fears of the unknown or the Other, so until the Modernist period it favoured a socially acceptable outcome that reassured the reading public. This policy forced authors, even female and feminist ones such as Kate Chopin, either to tame their sensual shrews or to kill them off prematurely. In *Jude the Obscure* Sue punishes herself for unwifely behaviour and Jude has to die for presuming to aim to cross class boundaries from scarecrow to Oxford scholar. Lawrence and Forster treat their women a bit more kindly than Hardy, but they make it clear that society and family do not approve of forward women, like Helen in *Howard's End*, Lucy in *A Room With a View* and Ursula and Gudrun in *Women in Love*, all of whom are criticised for daring to be different.

The social assumptions relating to class, gender and race that are inherent in novels of the eighteenth to the early twentieth centuries — by Defoe, Austen, Dickens, Hardy and Hartley — are part of the 'great tradition' of English Literature. Such prolific authors in the most popular literary genre had a huge influence on the perpetuation of stereotypical behaviour. Below are some of the unquestioned mores and beliefs conveyed in their works:

- Success is assessed according to wealth.
- Marriage is the only desirable state.
- Women must find a man to marry them.
- Women take their husband's name on marriage.
- Marriage must be within the same social class.

- Your community will reject you if you try to move social groups.
- Women need to know how to sew and play the piano.
- Women must wait to be asked to dance, go on a date or get married.
- Unquestioning patriotism is admirable.
- You should always be grateful to a benefactor.
- Girls do not need to go to school, but their brothers do.
- Too much education for girls is a bad thing and makes them unmarriageable.
- A pretty face is the most important attribute of a female.
- Women should not reveal their age.
- Marriage is for procreation; mistresses are for sexual pleasure.
- A male child is more desirable; a son and heir is necessary to perpetuate the family line.
- Men should be older than women in love relationships.
- Men should be taller than women in love relationships.
- Women should be seen but not heard, and when they do speak, they should do so softly and low.
- Servants should be devoted, loyal and invisible.
- British is best.
- People who step out of line morally or socially fall physically ill and often die.
- A woman's reputation must be preserved at all costs or her family will suffer.
- Elopement or adultery means social death.
- A large dowry is required for a good marriage.
- Sisters should look after their younger brothers.
- Foreigners cannot be trusted, nor can foreign words or names.
- The survival of the baby is more important than that of the mother giving birth.

Thus, even where nonconformist behaviour is shown by women in literature (as prescribed and judged by fathers, brothers and husbands), fatal punishment for such unnaturalness awaits them, by means of and therefore sanctioned by the natural elements of fire and water. In many cases this comes after years of being drugged or locked up as insane, to keep these unwomanly women isolated from decent society. (See Gilbert and Gubar's seminal work *The Madwoman in the Attic* and the Victorian short story, 'The Yellow Wallpaper' by Charlotte Perkins Gilman.) Medical discourse is harnessed to punish physical or mental transgression, and heroines fall seriously ill as a warning if they talk too much or reveal too much emotion publicly, as Marianne Dashwood does in *Sense and Sensibility*. Their only hope is to cross over to a world where the rules do not apply, so that Alice is liberated and able to be naughty with impunity in *Alice's Adventures in Wonderland* and *Through the Looking-Glass* — but then it turns out to be just a dream (and a male fantasy of prepubescent female naughtiness).

It is not only fictional males who disapprove of unfeminine behaviour and attitudes — summarised as a dangerous spirit of independence. Other women, older or uglier and therefore envious, willingly play the role of moral guardians and prison warders. They savagely condemn and reject the young women, even their own daughters or surrogate daughters, who threaten a status quo that provides their financial security, stemming from the social status of the males on whom they are dependent as housekeepers or wives, e.g. Juliet's nurse and Nelly in *Wuthering Heights*. The female victims also collude in their own punishment to the point of inflicting it upon themselves.

Privileged patriarchal readings

The Shakespeare and Shelley sonnets below make assumptions that demand a privileged reading. However they are read, there are not only no female roles but no suggestion that women exist. This applies to a surprising number of literary texts.

'Ozymandias' by P. B. Shelley

I met a traveller from an antique land
Who said: Two vast and trunkless legs of stone
Stand in the desert. Near them, on the sand,
Half sunk, a shattered visage lies, whose frown,
And wrinkled lip, and sneer of cold command,
Tell that its sculptor well those passions read
Which yet survive, stamped on these lifeless things,
The hand that mocked them, and the heart that fed:
And on the pedestal these words appear:
'My name is Ozymandias, king of kings:
Look on my works, ye Mighty, and despair!'
Nothing beside remains. Round the decay
Of that colossal wreck, boundless and bare
The lone and level sands stretch far away.

- 'I' is assumed to be male, because narrators are usually men.
- 'Traveller' is assumed to be male and educated, because it is an active role and in the public sphere.
- 'Desert' is a culturally exotic, distant place where strange things happen.
- 'Frown' and 'sneer' are the assumed right of the ruler over the ruled, taming and patronising from above.
- Patriarchal and colonial punishments are necessary to preserve order.
- 'Command' implies that the statue is male and confers god-like status, as God is male, men give commands, and women, natives and lower classes obey.
- 'Sculptor' is assumed to be male, as words ending in '-or' usually are; artists are male because they are licensed to look and have the gift of creation.

- 'These words appear' is a testament to maleness, the right to speak.
- 'Name' relates to the male power of language: Adam named the animals, white man named the natives, the male Church baptises, invaders rename conquered lands and men give their names (father or husband) to women and children.
- 'Kings' is privileged over 'queens', which are not equal; 'king of kings' is the highest status, with divine associations.
- 'Look' demands attention and admiration, the prerogative of males.
- 'My works' is a reference to the competitive male need to create and leave something tangible and eternal behind to cause 'despair' to other men.
- 'Mighty' and 'colossal' (and 'vast' in line 2) are male adjectives of size, suggestive of lands and armies; emperors and tribal leaders are assumed to be male.

Sonnet 18 by William Shakespeare
Shall I compare thee to a summer's day?
Thou art more lovely and more temperate:
Rough winds do shake the darling buds of May,
And summer's lease hath all too short a date:
Sometime too hot the eye of heaven shines,
And often is his gold complexion dimmed;
And every fair from fair sometime declines,
By chance, or nature's changing course untrimmed:
But thy eternal summer shall not fade,
Nor lose possession of that fair thou ow'st,
Nor shall death brag thou wand'rest in his shade,
When in eternal lines to time thou grow'st,
So long as men can breathe, or eyes can see,
So long lives this, and this gives life to thee.

- A male persona is doing the looking and comparing.
- Nature is the criterion against which beauty is judged.
- Balance and temperance are approved; extremes are not.
- Beauty, and therefore love, is ephemeral and endangered.
- 'Fair' is a physical and moral term of approbation, to be contrasted with dark and evil.
- Death is male and rapacious.
- Poets (male) have the gift of conferring eternal life.
- Heterosexuality is the assumption and privileged reading (though this sonnet is addressed to a young man).

Twentieth-century writers who tried to suggest that alternative codes of conduct were acceptable for women, such as D. H. Lawrence and James Joyce, had their books banned and ended their days in exile, having been denounced as shockingly immoral.

Social and historical bias

Obviously, feminist academics take a dim view of the marginalisation of women characters in literature and the low representation of women writers on specifications, especially when it is argued in response that this is because there have not been as many female writers as male during previous centuries. This is turning a blind eye not only to the amount of women's literature that has disappeared, but also to the social and cultural context of the late eighteenth to early twentieth centuries, in which women had little time and no privacy — 'no room of their own' — in which to write. The public attitude to women writers is indicated by their need to pretend to be male or use male pseudonyms for all or part of their writing career. This included Jane Austen ('A Gentleman'), the Brontë sisters (Currer, Ellis and Acton Bell) and George Eliot (Mary Ann Evans). If any of these five women had had wifely and motherly duties to fulfil, or less tolerant fathers, there may well have been no novels. Even today some women writers use their initials or a nickname to disguise their gender and prejudicial responses to it (Stevie Smith, U. A. Fanthorpe, A. S. Byatt).

Sylvia Plath failed to reconcile the roles of wife and mother with that of poet in the early 1960s. Women writers who made it into print were then often demeaned in various ways: accused of not having written it (Mary Shelley); of it having written itself (George Eliot); of it having been inspired by the man she was living with (Elizabeth Browning). The woman writer has been accused of not really being a woman or of not really being a writer, and if all else fails, of being immoral (Charlotte Brontë): *Jane Eyre* was described as being a masterpiece if written by a man, shocking or disgusting if written by a woman.

There is a 'Catch-22' in trying to remedy the imbalance of representation of class, gender and race. Although former colonies have generally achieved cultural independence, if post-colonial writers wish for a wide reading or theatre audience, they must write in English, even though the cultural imperialism of the English language may be what they wish to attack. These writers are thereby ironically aiding and abetting an unacceptable tradition and attitude. Likewise many non-middle-class authors have broken into the publishers' lists at the risk of then being viewed as having betrayed their working-class origins and loyalties; women writers may find themselves ghettoised on all-female prize nomination lists.

Alternative readings

The role of the contemporary literature student who wants to be aware of how text is biased and how readers are complicit in the construction of privileged readings is to question and deconstruct all text, to map the silences in order to identify the assumptions and exclusions. Ask yourself how feminist, Marxist or post-colonial readings of H*amlet*, *Paradise Lost*, 'To His Coy Mistress', 'The Sick Rose', 'La Belle Dame Sans Merci', 'The Lady of Shalott' etc. would differ from the dominant patriarchal one. Margaret Atwood playfully suggests that if prejudicial readings were removed from texts this is what would happen: 'There was once a poor girl, as beautiful as she was good, who lived with her wicked stepmother' would become 'There was once a young person of indeterminate social background, as average-looking as he was well-adjusted, who lived with a surrogate parent of indeterminate gender and morality.' This absurd and extreme example still makes a point about needing to read between the lines and think about language bias.

The situation has begun to change: letters, diaries, journals, short stories, oral accounts, personal accounts, autobiographies — traditionally the more personal and previously ignored, female, black and working-class narrative genres — have now been included in the literary canon, and mother/daughter and other female relationships have come to the fore in contemporary women's writing. Whether these are the texts chosen by English departments for their students (especially their male students) to study, however, is another matter.

Cultural and historical context

The A-level assessment criteria require candidates to 'evaluate the significance of cultural, historical and other contextual influences on literary texts', and this aspect of literary studies carries up to a quarter of the total marks available at A-level. You should understand how AO5 is weighted and know in which units it is assessed for your exam board. Learning about context is essential to understanding the influences on the writing and contemporary reading of texts. You must make a conscious effort to show this knowledge in most of your coursework and exam essays. Below are examples of the information you need to know to be able to fulfil AO5:

- date of writing or publication and how this relates to the time in which the text is set
- name and main features of the literary period to which it belongs
- political context, e.g. dominant social theories, influence of the monarch, colonial rule
- social conditions, urban and rural; class, gender and racial roles and relationships
- prevailing cultural trends, fashionable ideas, habits and lifestyles, e.g. attitude to tanned skin
- dominant attitudes at the time to major concepts such as war, religion, marriage, suicide
- historical legacies — previous events or ideologies affecting the views in the text
- known influences — acknowledged debts by authors to other writers or philosophies

- position of the text in the author's own oeuvre — early, middle or late work and links to previous works
- borrowings of titles, characters or styles; sources of epigraphs and other quotations
- debt to literary traditions and origins, e.g. Romance, Bible, fabliaux
- possible designs on the reader in terms of propaganda or persuasion of some kind
- religious and legal restrictions on what could be included in texts at the time
- retractions or changes to endings made as a result of a change of heart or public pressure
- relationship between text and artistic movements of the period, e.g. pre-Raphaelite painting
- moral and psychological context; definitions of good and evil; fears and taboos
- attitudes to/treatment of nonconformity, e.g. sexual deviation, madness, atheism
- relevant major national or world events, e.g. moon landing, Hiroshima, First World War
- contemporary publications that disturbed previous convictions, e.g. Darwin's *On the Origin of Species*
- medical beliefs and practices, e.g. the cause of hysteria, use of leeches, herbal remedies
- family structures and practices, e.g. primogeniture, chaperones and dowries

It should not be assumed that a recent text shares present day values. The rate of cultural change accelerated so rapidly during the latter part of the twentieth century that references to the 1960s, for example in the poetry of Carol Ann Duffy, may be more obscure and inaccessible than those to the Victorian period, because this decade is not covered in school history curricula. No amount of background knowledge, however, can be a substitute for a close focus on the content and language of the set text. The purpose of contextual knowledge is to lead you towards meaning through providing a relevant perspective and to enable you to relate your information to different texts produced under similar conditions or to similar texts produced under different conditions. Although literature is produced by humans at their most individual, writers are simultaneously and necessarily under the influence of the times they live in.

Approaching drama

Drama is the oldest genre of literature and is still going strong, though Plato wanted it banned, Puritans closed theatres in the seventeenth century, and it was predicted in the twentieth century that live drama would be killed off first by film, then by television and then by video. It continues to exert the same fascination on audiences, however, as it did in 500 BC in the city-state of Athens, where drama flourished with annual spring festivals (dedicated to Dionysus) of three tragedies and a satyr play in a row. The tickets were subsidised under Pericles so that the poor could also attend and acquire an appropriate habit of mind, dramatists then being considered to be the moral teachers of the people. In its earliest form drama was simply a chorus, a group of ordinary people dressed identically who, by chanting and dancing, reacted to a tragic situation. Later, individual actors were added, and a comedy genre was developed.

Popular appeal

The great flowering of the Elizabethan and Jacobean theatre in England presents a picture of total popular interest and participation — no Londoner was more than two miles from a playhouse — despite the fact that audiences had to suffer perform-ances outdoors in all weathers. Because literacy was not required and the stories were familiar, everyone could follow and appreciate a theatrical performance.

The theatre is a debating chamber for current and perennial moral issues and can cause life-changing mental as well as physical reactions in the audience, such as crying or laughing. Drama is a public event that clarifies private thought and enables us to feel a member of society in the sharing of the humour or the horror. The didactic element is present because, as Freud pointed out, it is natural to personify and dramatise what people do not understand but want to understand. By witnessing events and passions on stage we can experience, more immediately and intimately than with prose or poetry, what life has to offer. Drama is by definition generated by conflict (which creates the tension, the motivational force for the audience), and it is therefore the appropriate genre in which to clash the great moral issues, such as revenge versus law or good versus evil. The medieval morality play was a primitive tussle between angels and devils for Everyman's soul, and this is still the basic but more sophisticated dramatic format in the continuing exploration of what it is to be human.

A playwright has to write consciously for the theatre — since the work will not endure or remain in print if not performed — in a more imperative way than poets or novelists have to take account of their readers. The audience is itself an active element in the performance of drama, affecting the atmosphere by its size, consti-tution and responsiveness, and making each performance slightly different in a way that causes critics to argue about whether drama is a true art form. Paradoxically, audiences need what they are witnessing to be real enough to convince, but if it is too mundanely similar to everyday life, as the genre of kitchen-sink drama is accused of being, we lose the thrill of escape and the incentive to go to the theatre. However, it is possible to portray psychological realism without surface or physical realism, as Beckett's works show, so that the situation, issues or language are recognisable, even though the actual environment or the characters (who may be supernatural or mythological) may not be.

Characteristics of drama

There are traditional 'willing suspensions of disbelief' required of theatre audiences, e.g. actors talking to themselves. Characters are in a constant state of restless movement and unable to sit still for more than a few seconds, since drama has to be dynamic to give the audience something to watch as well as something to listen to. It is also an unquestioned artificiality of drama that time lapses of anything between minutes and years occur between acts and scenes, and that we have been transported to a different room, town or country by the changing of a set.

Serious modern drama tries to avoid such simplistic categorisations as comedy and tragedy, and alternates the two moods (a technique used by Tom Stoppard), leaves the ending open or ambiguous, or only partially resolves the problem. However, some sense of closure is necessary to complete the dramatic experience.

Drama is the product of a conflict that leads to a climax and can be created by:

- sudden change of roles or routine
- competition or power struggle
- family disagreement or problem
- misunderstanding between married partners
- betrayal between friends
- political crisis demanding an immediate response
- love triangle
- gender, class, race or generation battle
- 'duty versus desire' dilemma within an individual
- crisis of conscience caused by guilt or secret knowledge
- clash between alienated individual and social context
- opposing attitudes or beliefs between a couple or within a group
- an act of injustice precipitating revenge
- arrival of an outsider who acts as a catalyst
- an accusation that polarises family or community

Tension is what the audience experiences while watching the unfolding of the conflict and which becomes acute at the point of climax. Devices used by a playwright to make the audience feel apprehensive and engaged include:

- dramatic irony — a character making what the audience knows to be an unwise decision
- stretching out an agonising moment
- soliloquy or sharing of pain with the audience
- admission of guilt or a secret that will have consequences
- time pressure, deadline or ultimatum
- the suggestion that fate is against the character(s)
- knowing that a character will be devastated or furious when he or she finds out something

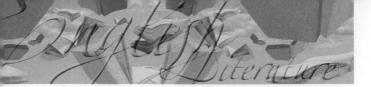

- established character deciding to leave
- new character arriving unannounced
- waiting for something or someone
- audience feeling torn between the conflicting rights of two characters
- threats, curses and prophecies
- use of sound effects, particularly bad weather and screams
- use of pauses in delivery of speeches, or silence on stage
- raising of voices, or speaking simultaneously
- whispering, hissing or any changes from normal use of voice
- actions performed clandestinely without knowledge of other characters
- body language or use of objects to symbolise disturbed mental states
- antipathy or antagonism between characters
- change in a character's behaviour, dress mode or expression
- unexplained mystery or unanswered question

Resolution is the solving of the problem that led to the conflict. It may take the form of:
- marriage or reunion of couple
- death or reprieve from death
- return to status quo
- change of perception, or a renunciation, to allow shared viewpoint
- explanation of a misunderstanding
- battle won or lost
- admission of a lie
- withdrawal of a threat
- revelation of a secret
- explanation of a mystery
- an act of justice
- departure of troublemaker
- granting of freedom
- farewell and journey
- family reunion

Dramatic effect

The first rule of responding to a drama text is to refer to the audience, not to the reader. Drama is the spoken and not the printed word, and can only be fully appreciated in performance since it also involves gestures, movements, stage positions and groupings, as well as the physical appearances of character and setting. Drama should be treated differently from poetry or prose texts, with reference made to visual elements and the effect of stage directions, including those relating to lighting and set in more modern works, such as Friel's *Translations*.

Essay questions often ask for an analysis of the dramatic effect of parts of a set drama text, and students are sometimes unsure what this means. In this context, 'dramatic' does not just mean exciting or violent, as it tends to in colloquial expression. The literary meaning of 'dramatic' pertains to the representation of conflict and the creation of tension. You need to analyse the scene in terms of its use of surprise, irony, emotion and the relationship between characters on stage, as expressed in dialogue, tone of voice, facial expression and body language. Unlike in narrative, actors can speak while simultaneously performing an action (in a novel it would have to take the sequential form of '"I hate you!" she shouted as she hit him'), which intensifies the effect.

As it is unusual for all characters in a play to be present on stage at once — except perhaps in the concluding scenes of a comedy — you need to be aware of entrances and exits and clear in your mind who is present at any particular point. Even when present, characters can share a stage but not relate to each other, with one or more silently watching, or one having the lion's share of the dialogue. The position of characters on stage and the groups they form are an important means of revealing attitudes and relationships, and of suggesting solidarity, communication breakdown or antagonism. It is crucial to note and interpret stage directions as well as dialogue, and many playwrights, such as Tennessee Williams and Brian Friel, reveal a lot about characterisation and theme in their stage directions, which go beyond just indicating physical movement.

Seeing a performance of a work can change your views of it radically. It can also clarify a point of dispute or reveal a new aspect of the work. This makes it highly desirable for you to see a theatrical production of your set text, or at least a film version.

Approaching poetry

The poetry module may be the one that you find most daunting, because it is the one with which you are least familiar in your private reading. The danger lies in treating poetry as prose — in searching for a chronological or narrative meaning, as you would with fiction — and ignoring the fact that poetry can be abstract, ambiguous, contradictory, condensed or allusive and can use poetic licence to break any rules it wishes. Poetry is meant to be heard, and sound is therefore a major consideration.

Defining poetry

The following have been suggested as definitions of poetry. Consider the appropriateness of each. Poetry is:

- 'the spontaneous overflow of powerful feelings...recollected in tranquillity' (Wordsworth)

- 'the best words in the best order' (Coleridge)
- something inspired for which the poet is only a medium
- the only way of dealing with abstract and spiritual subjects
- 'a momentary stay against confusion' (Robert Frost)
- 'What oft was thought, but ne'er so well expressed' (Alexander Pope)
- something that doesn't really make sense close up
- 'an imaginary garden with real toads in it' (Marianne Moore)
- the capture of the essence of things
- a way of seeing familiar things in unfamiliar ways
- 'what the world is made of' (Simon Armitage)
- 'conceived and composed in the soul' (Thomas Gray)
- something that must come as naturally as 'leaves to a tree' (Keats)
- that which is 'overheard' (J. S. Mill)
- 'the record of the best and happiest moments of the happiest and best minds' (Shelley)
- 'something more philosophic and of graver import than history' (Aristotle)
- 'the achievement of the synthesis of hyacinths and biscuits' (Carl Sandburg)
- ordinary language used in extraordinary ways
- making universal meanings from personal particulars
- weaving the old threads of language into a new and dazzling cloth
- that which 'sinks to the most primitive and forgotten, returns to the origin and brings something back' (T. S. Eliot)
- tones that existed 'before words were, living in the cave of the mouth' (Robert Frost)
- language being worked hard
- an occasion of truth, the place where it becomes tellable
- a congruence of time, place and emotion
- language with the safety-catch removed

Two poetic definitions of poetry are given in the following extracts.

From 'Ars Poetica' by Archibald MacLeish

A poem should be palpable and mute
As a globed fruit…

A poem should be wordless
As the flight of birds…

A poem should be motionless in time
As the moon climbs…

A poem should not mean
But be

'Prose Poem Towards a Definition of Itself' by Brian Patten

When in public poetry should take off its clothes and wave to the nearest person in sight; it should be seen in the company of thieves and lovers rather than that of journalists and publishers. On sighting mathematicians it should unhook the algebra from their minds and replace it with poetry; on sighting poets it should unhook poetry from their minds and replace it with algebra; it should touch those people who despise being touched; it should fall in love with children and woo them with fairytales; it should wait on the landing for two years for its mates to come home then go outside and find them all dead.

When the electricity fails it should wear dark glasses and pretend to be blind. It should guide all those who are safe into the middle of busy roads and leave them there. It should scatter woodworm into the bedrooms of all peg-legged men, not being afraid to hurt the innocent or make such differences. It should shout EVIL! EVIL! from the roofs of the world's stock exchanges. It should not pretend to be a clerk or a librarian. It should be kind, it is the eventual sameness of contradictions. It should never weep until it is alone, and then only after it has covered the mirrors and sealed up the cracks.

Poetry should seek out pale and lyrical couples and wander with them into stables, neglected bedrooms, engineless cars, unsafe forests, for a final Good Time. It should enter burning factories too late to save anyone. It should pay no attention to its real name.

Poetry should be seen lying by the side of road accidents, hissing from unlit gas-rings. It should scrawl the nymphomaniac's secret on her teacher's blackboard; offer her a worm saying: Inside this is a tiny apple. Poetry should play hopscotch in the 6pm streets and look for jinks in other people's dustbins. At dawn it should leave the bedroom and catch the first bus home to its wife. At dusk it should chat up a girl nobody wants. It should be seen standing on the ledge of a skyscraper, on a bridge with a brick tied around its heart. It is the monster hiding in a child's dark room, it is the scar on a beautiful man's face. It is the last blade of grass being picked from the city park.

(Reprinted by permission of HarperCollins Publishers Ltd. © Brian Patten 1995)

Poetic form

As can be seen in the Patten 'prose poem', and in the examples below, the borderline between prose and poetry is narrow, and line breaks, or the lack of them, can seem arbitrary.

From 'A Step Away From Them' by Frank O'Hara

It's my lunch hour, so I go
for a walk among the hum-colored
cabs. First, down the sidewalk

where laborers feed their dirty
glistening torsos sandwiches
and Coca-Cola, with yellow helmets
on. They protect them from falling
bricks, I guess. Then onto the
avenue where skirts are flipping
above heels and blow up over
grates. The sun is hot, but the
cabs stir up the air. I look
at bargains in wristwatches. There
are cats playing in sawdust.

From *Under Milk Wood* by Dylan Thomas

Herring gulls heckling down to the harbour where the fishermen spit and prop the
morning up and eye the fishy sea smooth to the sea's end as it lulls in blue. Green
and gold money, tobacco, tinned salmon, hats with feathers, pots of fish-paste,
warmth for the winter-to-be, weave and leap in it rich and slippery in the flash and
shapes of fishes through the cold sea-streets. But with blue lazy eyes the fishermen
gaze at that milkmaid whispering water with no ruck or ripple as though it blew
great guns and serpents and typhooned the town.

Although sound — including rhyme, rhythm and repetition — is important to
poetry's meaning, so is form, which can be appreciated only on the printed page,
so that line lengths, enjambement, stanza breaks, solo lines, typography and visual
symbolism can be fully appreciated. This is demonstrated through the form of the
following poem by Roger McGough.

'40–LOVE' by Roger McGough

40 –	LOVE
middle	aged
couple	playing
ten	nis
when	the
game	ends
and	they
go	home
the	net
will	still
be	be
tween	them

(From *After the Merrymaking* © Roger McGough 1971.
Reproduced by permission of PFD on behalf of Roger McGough)

Word order

Whether a poem has a regular metre can be ascertained by counting the number of syllables per line, but to know which metre it is you need to mark the stressed and unstressed syllables in several of the lines to see if there is a regular pattern, using the conventional notation of / for stressed (strong) syllables and ~ for unstressed (weak) syllables, placed above the syllable. The examples below cover a range of traditional poetic metres used in English verse.

- trochee (/~): suggestive of childish utterance or incantation

  / ~ / ~ / ~ / ~
  Double, double toil and trouble;
  / ~ / ~ / ~ / ~
  Fire burn, and cauldron bubble.

- anapaest (~~/): suggestive of rapidity of movement; galloping

  ~ ~ / ~ ~ / ~ ~ / ~ ~ /
  And the sheen of their spears was like stars on the sea.

- iamb (~/): suggestive of naturalness and confidence

  ~ / ~ / ~ / ~ /
  For though I'll pass from off the earth,
  ~ / ~ / ~ / ~ /
  My features will enjoy re-birth...

- dactyl (/~~): suggestive of mourning or haunting

  / ~ ~ / ~ ~ / ~ ~ / ~ ~
  Blow the wind, blow the wind, blow the wind southerly

If poetry is 'the best words in the best order' (Coleridge), it is important to look at the order as well as the words. Experimenting with different orders reveals the significant contribution made by rhythm and syntax to meaning. The metre, if there is one, imposes limitations, but on the other hand poetic syntax is more flexible than that of prose. This is the opening of Gray's 'Elegy Written in a Country Churchyard', written in iambic pentameter — the most common of metres in English poetry (and Shakespeare's plays) — and alternate rhyme:

> The curfew tolls the knell of parting day,
> The lowing herd winds slowly o'er the lea,
> The ploughman homeward plods his weary way,
> And leaves the world to darkness and to me.

The words in line 3 can be rearranged in many ways to fit the metre and still make sense, but the emphasis and effect would be slightly different in each case:

- 'The ploughman weary plods his homeward way' — emphasis on 'weary' created by the inversion of noun and adjective and by internal echo between 'weary' and 'way'.
- 'The ploughman weary his way homeward plods' — visual connection of 'weary' and 'way', and stress on the arduousness of the journey because of the delayed verb.
- 'His weary way the ploughman homeward plods' — the alliteration on 'w' and the inverted subject emphasise the negative adjective 'weary'.
- 'His homeward way the weary ploughman plods' — this line emphasises the positive adjective 'homeward'.
- 'The weary ploughman his way homeward plods' — here the emphasis is on 'plods', created by the delayed verb.
- 'The ploughman plods his weary homeward way' — alliterative 'p', the double adjective qualifying 'way' and the prosaic word order stress his daily routine.

Preparing poetry texts

It is probably not possible, or necessary, in the time available to cover all of the poems in your set-text collection, and your teacher will have selected a range of poems for you to study that includes examples of all the styles, genres, themes, periods, viewpoints and moods of your poet or anthology. As you study each poem, pay close attention to its title and final lines, which will help you with aim and meaning. Never assume that the speaker/persona in a poem is the poet, though it may be. If previous versions of any poems are known to exist, as with Keats and Owen for example, it can be enlightening to compare them with the final version. Be aware of intentional or unintentional ambiguity, which may occur in the identity or personality of the speaker, in the situation, or in the tone. Many hours have been spent in literature lessons debating the mood of the end of Hardy's 'The Darkling Thrush', the decision taken at the end of Robert Frost's 'Stopping by Woods on a Snowy Evening', or the meaning of Blake's epigram 'Better murder an infant in its cradle/Than nurse unacted desires', or the speaker of the final three lines of Keats's 'Ode on a Grecian Urn'.

When you have annotated and discussed each poem, think about which other poems in the collection it compares or contrasts with, so that when you have finished your studies you can group the poems, both thematically and stylistically, to help you to remember them and to decide how they could be used for coursework or the exam. At the revision stage you will probably decide on six to eight poems that you and your teacher consider particularly representative of the poet or period, and therefore most useful for exam purposes, and these will be the ones you will get to know particularly well. Exam essay practice and class discussion will help to fix some of the quotations in your mind, and will have introduced you to the kind of question most likely to be asked about your poetry selection.

Writing poetry essays

Whether for coursework or in response to a set text, poetry essays need especially careful consideration: you may have to choose which poems to use, and a wise choice is crucial to the success of the response; the poems you particularly like or know best may not be the most suitable for a particular essay question and you must be prepared to be flexible. However, a title that asks you to focus on a particular number of poems does not preclude your making passing reference (if strictly relevant) to other poems as additional support. Another challenge is to find a way of structuring a response that refers to several poems but does not seem incoherent, fall into separate critical commentaries or repeat itself. Generally the integrity of the essay is provided by your argument, based on the keyword(s) in the question, focused on themes or style, and for which the individual poems provide mixed support for each point. Plan the essay according to what the poems have in common in relation to the title, and use the shared characteristics for the topic/paragraph headings.

With poetry particularly you are expected to use short quotations within every sentence. There are also many literary terms to describe poetic devices, and it is to your credit to be able to identify and name these usages, provided that you incorporate them into your interpretation or argument and explain the effect they have created, rather than just mentioning them without analysis. (A glossary of literary terms and concepts is given on pp. 154–67.)

Approaching prose

Whether for coursework or exam, you will be studying a full-length novel at some point in your A-level course, and probably two: one pre- and one post-1900. On the whole, students feel more confident with novels than with drama and poetry, because narrative prose is the mode with which they are most familiar. However, the study of and response to novels requires particular skills and approaches because of their length and breadth, and because of the need to recognise how basic raw material is exploited according to the conventions of the genre. For instance, if you were to want to turn *Sleeping Beauty* into a horror story, you would focus on the evil fairy; if it were a romance you would focus on the prince and the rescue; if it were a mystery you would focus on the castle with the secret attic and the spinning wheel.

What is a novel?

Originally called 'novel' because it was a new genre — being a comparatively late arrival to the English literary scene in the early eighteenth century — the first novels were aimed at middle-class women who spent most of their lives at home with time to read. (There is still a gender divide in novel readership, with most males viewing fiction as less instructive and worthwhile than nonfiction; only 20% of library budgets is spent on fiction.) As an attempt at realism, the first novels had causally interlinked character and plot, and detailed descriptions of interior and exterior settings, costumes, vehicles, meals and other aspects of daily life.

E. M. Forster said that a novel is a succession of events arranged 'in their time sequence' until what Golding called 'a satisfactory end-point' is reached. This is not true of postmodern novels, and it would therefore be safer to use Atwood's definition of a novel being 'about somebody moving through time', or that of Carol Shields who said, 'a novel…is a story about the destiny of a child'. Novels are vehicles fuelled by curiosity, and if the reader does not want to know what happens next, they have stalled and failed as a means of transport. Because this genre can enter the minds of one, some or all of the characters in turn, reading a novel can be a complex and engaging experience, and one for which great claims have been made. Golding said (in his speech of acceptance for his Nobel Prize for Literature):

> There is no other medium in which we can live for so long and so intimately with
> a character…. It performs no less an act than the rescue and the preservation of
> the individuality and dignity of the single being…. No other art…can so thread
> in and out of a single mind and body, so live another life.

Traditional narrative presupposes a speaker/writer who communicates to a reader, in continuous prose, a series of events in chronological order. Postmodernist authors are at pains to subvert those expectations and passive way of reading by mixing genres and styles, narrators and viewpoints, facts and fiction, different interpretations of the same events and alternative outcomes — any device to force us to read actively and to question our assumptions about what text is. A novel can therefore now only safely be described as an extended fictional prose narrative, often divided into chapters or sections, which concerns a group of characters, some principal and some subsidiary, who may or may not be related, and a series of events, clearly or only implicitly connected, taking place now or over a period of time as short as a day or as long as several centuries, set in one or more defined or undefined places, more or less defined. It will usually be narrated in the first or third person, and may include some dialogue, reflection and description. It will have structure and integrity of some kind, more or less discernible, and there will be themes that act as a signal of recurring movement through time and the emotional and intellectual focus of the text. It may belong to a recognisable genre, such as social comedy, romance or horror, but may equally be a mixture of several.

Studying a novel

It makes sense to read the novel during the school holiday before your lessons in order to get a general picture of its genre and setting, characters and events, themes and style, and to form your first, uninfluenced, impressions. You will normally be provided with some background information prior to a detailed study of the novel, which may include relevant facts about the author, the period, the genre and the novel itself. While the novel is being studied in class you can reread it more closely, annotate the text, discuss the issues that arise, and prepare responses in the form of chapter summaries, character sketches, and theme and symbol lists. These are ways of observing and forming views on all the aspects and issues of the text, and will prove useful for later revision. Different types of essay questions or coursework title choices can be set when the textual study and annotation are complete or nearing completion.

Student activities

These activities enable you to engage with your set-text novel and get to know it in the kind of detail expected for a high grade at A-level.

Genre

- A romance can lead to either a comic or tragic outcome, but other genres are more predetermined, such as detective stories (the criminal will be discovered and justice will be done) and fairy tales (ending happily ever after). Genres of narrative have fixed plot lines and underlying structures. For example, in medieval fantasy there will always be a brave and intelligent but naive little man/orphan, a not-very-bright but devoted helper, an out-and-out villain, a kind relative/friendly magician, and there will be a sequence of battles between good and evil and good will finally win (see *Lord of the Rings*). Their characters do not matter, only their function, which is not negotiable, e.g. the helper cannot go over to the villain's side. What is the underlying genre of your novel, and how does it conform to the traditional available roles, structures and conventions?

- Incongruity of character, behaviour or language will trigger a realisation that a code is being breached which the reader would otherwise happily go on taking for granted. Is there any part of your novel where you feel this 'jarring'? Defamiliarisation can also take the form of self-referential authorial intrusion to remind the reader that this is a fiction, or of offering several possible endings or interpretations, thereby abdicating responsibility for the text. When a character in Shakespeare's *Twelfth Night* says, 'If this were played upon the stage now, I could condemn it as an improbable fiction', an extra dimension of irony is being created intertextually. What exactly is the code that is or is not being breached in your novel?

- If one or more television or feature-film versions of the novel exist, which will usually be the case with classics, they can be safely viewed only after you have acquired a close familiarity with the written text and have confidence in your own interpretation of it. Notes taken and tasks completed while you watch the film ensure that you are viewing actively and critically, constantly comparing the production with the text. This can usefully be followed by consideration of the significance of the divergences: absent characters, missing scenes, cut speeches, rearranged order of events, different ending or changed emphasis. The casting also rarely coincides with a reader's view of a character's appearance or personality. Consideration of why the director made these decisions and changes can add to an understanding of the actual text and raise awareness of other readers' interpretations. Remember it is only one director's interpretation of the text, not a definitive one, and has no more authority than your own.

- Make a plan for your own film of the novel, selecting scenes to be retained, characters who can be dispensed with, actors to be cast, opening and closing camera shots, and appropriate soundtrack music.
- Write a new final chapter or ending for the novel. Then write a commentary to explain your reasoning and choices, comparing your version to the text.

Themes

- Think about your novel's title. Were others considered (e.g. *Pride and Prejudice* was originally *First Impressions*)? How does the title set up comic or tragic expectations? Is it eponymous? Where does it place emphasis? Is it ironic or symbolic? Is it a pun, like *Hard Times* or *Enduring Love*, and if so what are the different meanings? Is it a quotation, like *Brave New World*, and if so how does it connect the novel to the original source? Is it allusive to another author and genre, like *The Handmaid's Tale*? Is it used by a character or by the narrator within the novel, and if so in what context? How does it relate to the overall themes of the novel? Is there another title that would have done as well, or better? Does the novel have a subtitle (Victorian ones often do) or an epigraph, and if so what does it imply? What subtitle or epigraph would you give the novel?
- List your novel's themes and design a diagram that relates them to each other.

Plot

- Is there a framework story or myth being exploited or another text implied? What difference would it make to the novel if it were not there?
- Italo Calvino, a postmodernist writer, says, 'In ancient times a story could end only in two ways: having passed all the tests, the hero and the heroine married, or else they died. The ultimate meaning to which all stories refer has two faces: the continuity of life, the inevitability of death.' How does this analysis relate to your novel?
- Did your novel originally have a different ending (often the case with Victorian novels) and if so, how, when and why was it changed, and with what effect?
- Write down some questions left unanswered by the novel. Think about why the reader has not been given the answers to these particular questions.

Character

- Consider the names of the characters; what do they suggest? In pre-1900 novels particularly they may indicate whether the character is to be admired or regarded as silly or wicked. Indicative or moral naming still continues in a more subtle fashion in modern and postmodern works, e.g. a female character may be given an exotic and therefore seductive name, or one from the Bible, with connotations of chastity (Marian in *The Go-Between* is meant to be an ironic composite of the Virgin Mary and Maid Marian, and Leo is both the ill-fated child of the zodiac and would-be lion king; Hardy's Arabella is too exotic for Jude, himself named very indicatively after the patron saint of lost causes). Do the characters in your novel have diminutives or nicknames used by other characters, and how does this add to characterisation?

- What are the main methods of characterisation? Think about which ones are conveyed mostly through description, interior monologue, dialogue, authorial comment, comment by other characters, imagery and symbols. Do any of the characters have catch phrases? Are any characters associated with particular places or objects?

- Are there any caricatures or stereotypical characters in your novel? Divide the characters in your novel into those for whom the reader has sympathy and those whom we are inclined to dislike or disapprove of. How has the reader been steered towards these responses?

- Does your novel have more than one main character or protagonist? Would you describe any of them as a hero or heroine? Is there discernible change in any character during the course of the novel? What has he or she learnt?

- Are there any characters who appear to contradict the main theme or stance of your novel, e.g. those who are apparently condemned but seem attractive to the reader, or who are meant to be individual but come across as stereotypes?

- Are any characters referred to but not seen or heard? What effect does this have?

Setting

- List the locations — towns, buildings, rooms and outside settings — used in the novel and analyse their contribution to its overall mood and atmosphere. Do any of them have a symbolic function, or employ the technique of pathetic fallacy, e.g. Wuthering Heights, Mansfield Park or Coketown.

- Draw a map of the one or more locations of your novel, labelling places mentioned and recording the events that occur there. Include all significant information, such as boundaries, geographical features, journey routes, shapes and relative sizes of buildings.

- Is there a prevalent or dominant season, month, time of day or type of weather in the novel? If so, how do they contribute to the genre, mood, atmosphere and reader expectation?

Structure

- If your novel is divided into sections as well as chapters, or has chapter titles as well as numbers, study the effect of these on structure. Is there a pattern to the chapter headings? Are there any recurring keywords or concepts within the chapter or section titles? What is the purpose of the divisions?
- A novel, because it is long and perhaps amorphous, uses recurrence to give it integrity, as in a musical symphony. This may be the reappearance of a certain symbolic character or object, repeated events, recurring language, or reference to theme. Can you identify what gives integrity to the novel you are studying?
- Can the novel be expressed in diagrammatic form, e.g. interlocking triangles, concentric circles, parallel or converging lines, a staircase?
- Does your novel have a framing device (as in *Wuthering Heights*)? How much time passes within the span of the novel? Where in the novel are there time jumps, previews or flashbacks? What is their effect? Is there a double time scheme, and if so what is its purpose? Are there changes of tense between past and present?
- Look at any logical or numerological patterns in the way the novel is divided, as in *Hard Times*. The order in which material is presented is itself sending a message through such devices as priority, connection, juxtaposition, cancelling, repetition, symmetry or circularity. What links one chapter or section to the next? Out of context, how might a reader misinterpret a single chapter?

Style

- Style is often a neglected element of novels, because students feel more confident discussing character and plot. However, character and plot themselves will not be the focus of exam or coursework questions, being superficial vehicles for the more important elements of theme and language. Identify both unusual and typical passages and analyse them first as unseen criticism, and then add in extra observations relating to intratextual context, e.g. repetition, recurring imagery, irony and contrast. This will give you a closer focus on the linguistic techniques of the novel and provide familiar passages for you to refer to in the exam or coursework.
- Analyse roughly the ratio of narration to dialogue, description and reflection, and comment on the effect of the proportions.
- Write an extra episode with dialogue for two or three of the main characters, aiming to capture their register and idiolect as well as typical content.

Narrative technique

- How would you describe the type of opening: intrigue, shock, *in medias res* (dialogue or action), or scene-setting?
- Novel openings usually introduce characters, themes, style, tone, imagery and expectation of future events, and can be the whole text in miniature. Study the

first two or three pages and analyse what is revealed about the way the novel will progress.

- Irony is a key element in character revelation and manipulation of reader response and is likely to be present in a prose fiction work of any period. Identify the comic or tragic situational ironies and unexpected reversals in the novel you are studying. Which characters, if any, use irony as a speech mode? Could the authorial voice or attitude be described as ironic?

- To what extent is your novel didactic? What is the message or attitude being conveyed to the reader? How subtle is the method of delivery? Is there any ambivalence about the meaning? Is there a character who seems to speak for the author?

- An area for focus in narrative is the use of dialogue. This mode enables characters to reveal — and often ironically to condemn — themselves out of their own mouths (e.g. the Eltons in *Emma*) and gives prose a quality of spontaneity and dramatised conflict, as well as a change from the narrative voice. Look at who gets to do the talking, and how much of it, and analyse how natural the dialogue seems. Is there any free indirect speech, as in Jane Austen, which blurs the distinction between authorial voice and character voice, usually for ironic effect?

- If your novel was originally a serial publication, like *Hard Times* and many other Victorian novels, look closely at the chapter endings to see how the 'cliff-hangers' are created.

- How intrusive is the authorial voice in your novel? Find passages of authorial presence or point of view or opinion, if they exist. Is the authorial voice also the narrative voice? Is the narration in the first or third person? Are there multiple narrators? What does your novel gain and lose by its choice of narrative stance, i.e. character narrator or omniscient author? If your novel has a naive narrator (e.g. Pip in *Great Expectations* and Leo in *The Go-Between*), what effect is achieved?

- Eighteenth-century novels were often epistolary (including the original version of *Pride and Prejudice*). Does your novel contain letters, and if so, what do they contribute?

- Novel endings are obviously significant, can be controversial, and are often the focus of an exam question. How does your novel's ending relate to everything that has gone before? What is left unexplained, unstated but implied, or completely open ended? Is there closure in any sense? Traditional eighteenth- and nineteenth-century novels tie up the loose ends and dispose of characters with marriage, death, miserable exile or happy retirement, according to their just deserts. Modernist novels tend to end with a symbolic and redeeming view of a better future world; contemporary novels are more likely to tell the reader nothing, in the name of realism, about what will happen next. Often it is not possible to tell even what frame of mind the main character is in at the end of the novel, which gives scope for readers to argue for their own interpretations. However, this kind of ending is very different from that which asks us to believe that the characters lived happily or unhappily ever after, and is more difficult to write about in that the lack of closure must be recognised and the different interpretations discussed and justified.

- Rewrite a section of narrative from a different viewpoint, and explain what has changed.
- Tell the plot or part of it from the perspective of a minor or marginalised character. This will help you to realise how the reader has been positioned to see and accept things from a particular perspective.
- Transform the genre of a particular section of the text. What difference does it make — and what light does it shed on the original choice of genre — to change a letter, for example, into a piece of reported speech or a dialogue into narrative?

Studying short stories

The genre of short stories originated in the nineteenth century, although it can be seen as a descendant of the poetry narratives of Chaucer's *Canterbury Tales*, in turn based on Boccaccio's prose stories written in the fourteenth century. The short story is analogous with traditional and modern oral narratives, many of them competitive within a social gathering, such as jokes, urban legends, sermons, ghost stories, gossip and anecdotes. Though one of the most prolific literary genres in the twentieth century (and continuing into the twenty-first), collections of short stories are less popular than novels with publishers, the reading public, exam boards and English teachers. It is less likely that critical support will exist for the study of short stories.

If you are studying a collection of short stories for an exam module, it is not advisable to approach them as mini-novels. Theme rather than character or plot is the way into the text, plus a close analysis of the narrator's role and how the reader is being positioned. There are fewer structural issues than with a novel, but the choice and organisation of material for an essay response are obviously more difficult for short stories than for a single prose text. As with poetry collections, the selection of stories to compare or contrast is crucial to the success of your argument. Some collections do not form a homogeneous whole in terms of content or style, and there is the added necessity of remembering different character names and plots, and of not confusing the titles and quotations that belong to each. Students need to examine the relationship between stories, as well as that between the part and the whole within each story. For instance, there may be a framing device that allows movement from an external to an internal narrator.

A short story usually fulfils the following definition: four or five printed pages dealing with one main character, but including up to three secondary speaking characters, to whom a life-changing, poignant and often ironic event occurs as an intensely observed moment of time. The master of the genre, Edgar Allan Poe, defined it as limited to 'a certain unique or single effect' and so tightly woven as to give a unity of impression with nothing extraneous or unnecessary to distract from it. The short story has a purity or distillation impossible in the novel — which tends to rely on a layering effect rather than a dramatic one — and involves the technique of ellipsis, a removal and reduction of information. However, what has been left out can be as significant as what has been included, requiring the reader to reconstruct from clues a character's previous experiences. Because of the need for compression, short stories usually contain only limited description and dialogue, with the focus mainly on narrative and feeling or reflection.

Short-story endings usually fall into one or more of the following categories: return to framework story; reference to a symbol; ironic comment by character or narrator; surprising twist; preview of future; change of point of view; repetition of an idea or situation but with a new significance. The twist-in-the-tale conclusion requires you to identify the stages and techniques leading up to it; paradoxically, the reader needs to be prepared for the ending as well as be surprised by it in order for it to have its full dramatic effect.

Typical themes of short stories are escape, or dreams thereof, and alienation (which are key themes of the modernist period in which the genre flourished). The lonely outsider — because of gender or nationality — is a common main character, and may be a useful starting point for analysing your set stories. You can also expect there to be an epiphany, a moment of insight in which, as E. M. Forster put it, 'the doors of heaven may be shaken open' and nothing can be the same again. Another way of describing this is as a 'frontier' experience, i.e. a crossing into new and disconcerting territory, where characters learn something about themselves, their way of life, or how others see them, which traumatically strips them of their naivety and false security. Because in some sense or other the main character is at a turning point or moment of maturity, where innocence becomes experience, short stories often have either children or childlike adults in this role.

Below are some useful activities for the study and revision of short-story set texts.

- Write a summary of each story in about 50 words. This will promote reflection on what the key aspects of the story are, how condensed it already is, and how much of the content of your summary is only implied in the story rather than stated.
- Consider the missing elements of the stories. What facts have not been given to the reader, and why? What has been left unsaid by a character or narrator? What unanswered questions is the reader left with? Do they matter?
- Study the title of each story, which will probably be between one and four words, with the aim of creating intrigue but not giving away too much. What do the titles

have in common? Do they refer to a character or event? Do any of them give a misleading impression of the content? Which, if any, suggest humour or irony? Which set up an expectation of tragedy? Does punctuation play a role in any of the titles?

- Identify whether the stories are first- or third-person narration. How would they have been different in the other person? Do they take a male or female point of view? Is the narrator omniscient and reliable, an internal or external character to the event, ignorant or naive? Is there a change of narrator within a story? How does the narrative viewpoint determine reader sympathy?

- Look closely at the openings and endings to the stories. If you removed the first sentence, how would the atmosphere, tone, characterisation or plot of the story be different? Categorise the type of ending each story employs; if an extra sentence were added to the ending, what difference would it make?

- How important is the setting in the story? Would it work equally well in another time period or location? Are weather, season or time of day significant in the creation of atmosphere? Is the collection as a whole aiming to create local colour?

- Underline the keywords — not more than ten — in each story. Notice also which words are repeated. Pick out one central image that you think dominates the story.

- Mark the turning point of the story, the climax of tension and any tone or style or viewpoint changes.

- The title story of a collection usually provides a focus for study and a link to the other stories. Place it at the centre of a spider diagram and label its relationship to all the other stories in the collection.

Approaching Shakespeare

Background

William Shakespeare was born in 1564 and died in 1616 (both on 23 April); he lived in Stratford-on-Avon and in London in the reigns of Elizabeth I and James I. He was married to an older woman with whom he had three children, one a twin called Hamnet, who died at the age of 11. Little is known about Shakespeare or his beliefs, and this paucity of information has led to speculation that someone may have borrowed his name, the main candidate being the contemporary playwright, atheist and homosexual, Christopher Marlowe. Shakespeare's plays show no consistent attitude to religion and marriage; however, authorship is irrelevant to the study of or response to his works. The plays were written between 1590 and 1612, and Shakespeare also wrote poetry, particularly sonnets. The 37 plays fall into the categories of comedy, tragedy, history (English and Roman) and what are known as the late plays or Romances.

His most famous plays are probably the four great tragedies written in the first decade of the seventeenth century. His final plays after *The Tempest* (1611) are thought to be collaborations. Different versions of the texts exist because the Quarto copies come from various unofficial sources, e.g. prompt scripts, whereas the Folio collection of 1623 was the first and posthumous publication of the complete plays (minus *Pericles*). All the dramatic works are believed to be based on earlier plays, short stories or historical references, which have all been identified except for the early comedies *A Midsummer Night's Dream* and *Love's Labours Lost*.

The comedies

The movement within a Shakespeare comedy is from initial problem through elaborate confusion to final resolution and a state of harmony; the dénouement usually involves the removing of disguise and the reunion of family members and lovers. Shakespeare comedies typically end with a triple wedding and feasting, singing and dancing, all of which are symbolic of unity. Many of them have a 'green world' location in a pastoral setting to contrast with the corrupt milieu of the court and city. Some of the plays are known as problem comedies because the resolution is partial, unconvincing or unsatisfactory, as in *Measure for Measure* and possibly *Twelfth Night*. The last group of comedies, influenced by a seventeenth-century taste for spectacle and music within drama, are also known as the Romances (or late plays) because of their dependence on magic, journeys, exotic locations, lost children and other trappings of fairy tales, a genre that ends justly and happily. Because high tension cannot be sustained relentlessly for more than two hours, and to serve as ironic juxtapositions to intensify feeling, there are comic scenes even in the tragedies. The aim of comedy is to make the audience think, and therefore learn, through the experience of watching characters make mistakes that we would not wish to make ourselves.

The tragedies

Tragedies develop from a serious early problem related to death, war or failure of judgement into a catastrophic situation requiring further deaths and noble sacrifices in order for the previous status quo, with new participants, to be restored. In the tragedies a move from the court to a contrasting place brings enlightenment, or at least an alternative viewpoint, as in *King Lear*, *Othello* and *Antony and Cleopatra*. There is a final anagnorisis, the recognition of an essential truth about something or someone. We are asked for our moral awareness, but not our moral judgement, since no one is in a position to judge fellow humans.

The tragic hero must be someone of importance within his own society and someone who has what Aristotle called a fatal (in both senses of the word) flaw. In Shakespeare this takes the subtle form of a seriously mistaken decision, taken freely and usually against advice, which starts off a disastrous, irreversible and seemingly inevitable chain of cause-and-effect events as the hero falls from high to low. The course that each tragic hero believes will lead to success in fact leads to destruction. The sense of waste and loss comes from the fact that the hero has superhuman qualities in other respects, or as Marlowe put it in the final chorus of *Dr Faustus*: 'Cut is the branch that might have grown full straight'. Because free will is applied, an accident of birth or fate alone cannot be blamed, making the dilemma more complex and a cause of concern to all humans with fears and desires.

The aim of tragedy is, through the inspiration of pity and fear (Aristotle's catharsis) to engage the audience's sympathies with the characters who are victims of their own weaknesses (or the evil of others or an apparently malignant fate), and to learn through identification with the tragic hero and to feel gratitude that we, who could so easily have been in the same situation, have been spared.

After the multiple body count (at least five, and nearly double in the case of *Hamlet*) and restoration, a survivor (usually a trustworthy character) makes the final chorus-type speech summing up the tragic events and looking forward to a brighter future; things can only get better. The audience is expected to feel purged by the extreme emotions of pity and fear it has been made to feel on another's behalf. Generally speaking it is a tragedy rather than a history play if we are asked to identify with the hero, because of his exceptional gifts, and if we care more about his sufferings than about the events or the period being represented on stage.

Themes

Obviously there are many sub-themes in such a wide corpus of work, but Shakespeare's main themes could be gathered under overall headings to do with the nature of good and evil, and cosmic relationships. The main questions the tragedies are asking are:

- What is a human being?
- Why are we here?
- Are humans in control of their own destiny?
- How can we tell right from wrong?
- What is nature and how does it relate to human nature?

The nature and role of women also concerned Shakespeare, as well as the bonds between family members, the difficulty of identifying truth, and political issues of power and succession.

Images

Theme and image are closely related in Shakespeare plays, and one is often the abstract version of the other, e.g. poison is a concrete image and represents the theme of corruption in *Hamlet*; Othello's blackness is a metaphor for evil but also his literal skin colour. Shakespeare's imagery therefore repays close study as being a key to the play and not just a descriptive aid or plot issue. It has been pointed out by Caroline Spurgeon that each play has its own peculiar and recurring group of images, and also that certain images are often found together in what she calls 'clusters', for instance dogs (especially spaniels) occur with fawning and flattery. In addition to Shakespeare's original imagery, the standard images of the Elizabethan period are also much in evidence, such as hell and heaven, light and dark, bonds and divisions.

Structure

All Shakespeare plays are now printed as five acts divided into a variable number of scenes, usually three or four but in some cases up to fifteen. The third act is likely to contain the climax of the dramatic tension. The plays, with a few exceptions including *The Tempest*, tend to follow only loosely the three classical unities of time, place and action, with parallel plots or subplots and scene changes occurring (in the comedies particularly). Some plays, like *Othello*, have double time schemes and others huge time jumps, such as the 16 years in *The Winter's Tale*. There may be an introductory chorus, as in *Romeo and Juliet*, or an epilogue in or out of character, as in *A Midsummer Night's Dream* and *The Tempest* respectively. The last scene will gather together all the characters, or as many as are still alive.

Form

Audiences do not notice or soon forget that they are listening to verse when they go to see a Shakespeare play because of all the devices used to subvert the regularity of the blank verse, such as couplets at the end of scenes for climactic or conclusive effect or for characters making highly significant or formal speeches. Prose is good enough for servants, peasants and clowns, and for higher-status characters when being underhand or off-duty. It is worth noticing where the changes from prose to verse and vice versa occur within a scene or one character's utterances, and to note any overall patterns, e.g. Othello's descent into unstructured prose from high-flown poetry under Iago's influence. Other devices to watch out for are the sharing and completing of each other's lines, which reveals something about the relationship, and the incomplete or half lines, which suggest a highly emotional state. In addition to these methods of giving the impression of natural dialogue, there are metrically irregular lines, the use of caesura and frequent enjambement. Plays may also contain songs, poems and letters to give variety and create mood, as well as to convey character and plot information.

Language

It is surprising how few words of a language written 400 years ago are unknown to students, despite their initial fears. It is more likely to be the elliptical or unusually ordered syntax that causes difficulties of immediate comprehension, but looking at phrases rather than individual words usually provides enough clues for meaning to be reasonably apparent. Certain words have, however, changed their meaning over time, wholly or partially, e.g. 'still' and 'presently', which then meant 'always' and 'immediately' respectively. Others are false friends, e.g. a 'mistress' was then a respectable member of society, hence our title 'Mrs'. In fact, most family titles have shifted, and 'cousin' and 'uncle' could be used more inclusively and less specifically then. Obviously you will want to write on your text the modern version of words that are central to an understanding of theme or character, but it is not necessary to gloss every unknown word and examiners have warned of the danger of over-annotation of Shakespeare texts in particular. Different versions of texts exist because the Quarto copies, derived from prompt-copies and early drafts, do not always exactly agree with each other or with the first posthumous publication of the plays in the Folio of 1623.

Theatrical conventions

Shakespeare was able to exploit certain classical theatrical conventions that a modern playwright could not easily get away with. Here are some examples.

- The use of trapdoors and balconies allowed hell and heaven to be represented in the theatre according to the convention that one is down and the other up.
- A character in disguise — although voices are very distinctive — is not recognisable by other characters, even relatives and spouses.
- An aside can be heard only by the audience, despite the other characters on stage being easily within earshot.
- A mortally wounded character takes an unrealistically long time to die, and manages to continue to speak cogently and at length until the last moment.
- Talking to oneself, otherwise known as soliloquy, is presented as a natural mode of discourse.
- In a soliloquy, the character speaking tells the truth about his or her thoughts and feelings.
- All actors were male and therefore female parts were played by boys (so a female character pretending to be a male involved an extra level of ironic confusion).
- Actors would routinely play more than one part and even major parts were sometimes doubled.
- Violent scenes usually took place off stage, for practical reasons, and were then reported on stage by messengers who witnessed them.

Changing attitudes

Treatment of Shakespeare's plays has changed over time. It would now be highly controversial to cast a white actor to wear black make-up to play Othello, and unthinkable to rewrite the ending of *King Lear*, as happened in the eighteenth century, to allow Cordelia and Lear to live. Dr Bowdler considered much of Shakespeare's language to be too sexually explicit and produced censored versions of the plays, which were still being used in schools in the latter half of the twentieth century. Until the Victorians invented the sentimental concept of the female fairy, they were always considered to be and played as male (as angels were). Modern audiences may perhaps read more into the term 'make love' than was intended, as it did not originally have a physical sense; and they wrongly assume that close same-sex relationships, where characters may declare their love for each other, have a homosexual dimension.

Some previously popular plays are now avoided because of perceived racist attitudes, particularly *The Merchant of Venice* for its depiction of Shylock, a Jew. Religious views have changed considerably since the early seventeenth century, when it was commonly believed that witches, ghosts and other evil spirits were active in luring humans to eternal damnation. The modern attitude to war is generally not consistent with the contemporary belief that it is unequivocally noble and glorious to be a soldier. However, it is the portrayal of women that provides the most debate among students studying Shakespeare today, and the social position of women is the most obvious difference in historical context between then and now.

Approaching unseen criticism

'Criticism' as a literary term means to provide a critique, rather than to find fault. Appreciation and appraisal are other words sometimes used instead, but they mislead in the opposite direction. The most accurate word for what you have to do with an unseen text for the final, synoptic module of A2 is 'analyse', i.e. provide an interpretation based on evidence. Although the poem or passage is unprepared, you should not be. This comes at the end of A2, counts for 20% of the total marks and is different from the other papers in that you have to show you are aware of how the different elements of literary studies — knowledge, skills and understanding — come together and support each other. Although it is the last unit, competence and confidence are acquired through continual practice, the development of habits and the experience of a wide range of genres and periods, so that unseen criticism should be a regular feature of the course from the beginning, especially since close analytical reading is the central skill required for all forms and levels of literary study. OCR teacher support material states that 'critical appreciation must play a significant part in every one of the units of the OCR specification', and this goes for the other exam boards too.

Having the skills to be able to see why particular devices create those particular effects, and being able to name them, is the essence of literary study and the common core of the Assessment Objectives. Unseen criticism is usually considered to be the most daunting component of an English Literature course, but it is really a matter of practice and confidence. No new skills are involved: you are already an experienced observer of texts and supporter of your views about them, and just need to transfer the existing skills you have already acquired from your study of set texts over several years. It is true, however, that unseen criticism distinguishes the candidate who can really understand literature independently from those who have conscientiously absorbed everything the teacher has said but are unable to perceive for themselves. This is why it is considered a higher-order skill and is assessed at the end of the A-level course.

Approaching an unknown text

There are no right answers, only plausible and implausible interpretations and, as with set texts, a convincing overview depends on your being able to provide sustained, detailed support consisting of close reference to the text. Do not paraphrase the content, narrate the plot or go through a checklist of literary terms and remark on their presence or absence. The aim is to show understanding of what the text — not the author — is saying and how particular effects have been achieved. Technical terms have their place, which is integrated into your definition and interpretation of the text, with an explanation of their purpose, as judged by their effect on the reader.

It is not helpful to approach a text with an intention to find a narrative (and paraphrase it), or to spot the themes and images (and list them), or to discern an allegorical meaning (and translate the symbols). Your response may include observations on these aspects, if they exist, but your approach should be a problem-solving quest that searches widely and deeply for evidence of how the piece has been shaped, without preconceptions or definitive conclusions.

Ambiguity

According to the poet and critic William Empson, 'the machinations of ambiguity are among the very roots of poetry'. How many ambiguities can you find in the sonnet below?

Sonnet 73 by William Shakespeare
That time of year thou may'st in me behold
When yellow leaves, or none, or few, do hang
Upon those boughs which shake against the cold,
Bare ruined choirs where late the sweet birds sang.
In me thou see'st the twilight of such day
As after sunset fadeth in the west;
Which by and by black night doth take away,

> Death's second self, that seals up all in rest.
> In me thou see'st the glowing of such fire,
> That on the ashes of his youth doth lie,
> As the death bed whereon it must expire,
> Consumed with that which it was nourished by.
> This thou perceiv'st, which makes thy love more strong,
> To love that well which thou must leave ere long.

The six possible readings (at least) of this sonnet are:

- speaker's reaction to approaching death
- protest against common attitudes to age
- rejection of Christian view of life after death
- comment on decline of Christianity
- achievement of immortality through poetry
- the power, pathos and ephemerality of love

Empson (in *Seven Types of Ambiguity*) quotes the line 'Bare ruin'd choirs where late the sweet birds sang' as an example of multiple meanings in poetry and argues that the effect of the line is created by the ambiguity, the different yet simultaneously possible interpretations:

- choirs, like birds, sit in rows with their mouths open
- old churches are often empty and in ruins
- 'bare' because prepubescent and without facial hair; innocent as children (choirboys)
- choir stalls are made of carved wood, i.e. from trees that used to house birds
- grey stone walls of churches are like a winter sky
- under Henry VIII, Elizabeth's father, the monasteries were stripped of their ecclesiastical ornaments and closed down when the religious orders were dissolved in the Reformation
- self-reference by Shakespeare to the winter of his life and a decline in his poetic powers

Irony

Most literary texts, and therefore poems and passages for unseen criticism, contain irony, as this is what gives the text its complexity and layering. Shelley's sonnet 'Ozymandias' (see p. 61), which you probably first came across at KS3 and understood on a superficial level, relies on both ambiguity and irony. There are several possible interpretations of 'Ozymandias':

- the god-like reproductive creativity of the artist
- the pointlessness of human endeavour
- the ugly face of dictatorship

- the capacity of time and the elements to destroy; the omnipotence of nature
- the vanity of human wishes; hubris

The main thing to notice about this poem is its use of multiple irony:
- there is actually nothing to admire
- the humble traveller is alive; Ozymandias the great man is not
- the statue meant to last for ever has fallen into ruin
- sand — the desert — is actually formed from disintegrated stone
- how 'mighty' Ozymandias would be the one to suffer 'despair' if he could see himself now
- what happens to people who sneer; pride comes before a fall
- there is no one to look upon these great 'works' anyway, in the middle of the desert
- even if there were 'mighty' spectators, they would not 'despair' out of awe, as intended
- Shelley's poem has outlived the statue, i.e. words last longer than stone
- kings are not omnipotent or more powerful than ordinary mortals; they just think they are
- how are the mighty fallen
- if this is a 'traveller's tale', there was probably never a statue anyway

You would also be expected to note the use of a framework, even in such a short text, i.e. the literary archetype of the travelling storyteller, and the use of quotation within direct speech within narrator's voice, to create levels of narration. There are three voices in the poem. It should be noted that the second sentence is 69 words long — whereas the third has only three — and has 19 punctuation marks. The negative suffix '-less' is used three times. The semantic field is one of body parts and destruction. The conjunction 'and' is used eight times and there are seven other words containing the same syllable, so that the sound echoes through the empty desert and the sonnet as a mockery of the name 'Ozymandias' (stressed correctly on the 'and'). The meaning and syntax of line 8 are obscure, but it has a certain suggestive power nonetheless. The sonnet can also be deconstructed for gender bias by a feminist critique (see p. 153). An intertextual irony is that Shelley plagiarised the idea for the poem from one by Horace Smith, which has not survived.

Sometimes irony can take the form of a deliberate mismatch between genre/form and content/diction, as in the sonnets below.

'On Home Beaches' by Les Murray
Back, in my fifties, fatter than I was then,
I step on the sand, belch down slight horror to walk
a wincing pit edge, waiting for the pistol shot
Laughter. Long greening waves cash themselves, foam change

sliding into Ocean's pocket. She turns: ridicule looks down,
strappy, with faces averted, or is glare and families.
The great hawk of the beach is outstretched, point to point,
quivering and hunting. Cars are the stuff at its back.
You peer, at this age, but it's still there, ridicule,
the pistol that kills women, that gets them killed, crippling men
on the towel-spattered sand. Equality is dressed, neatly,
with mouth still shut. Bared body is not equal ever.
Some are smiled to each other. Many surf, swim, play ball:
like that red boy, holding his wet T shirt off his breasts.

(Reprinted by permission of Les Murray)

'Mrs Noah: Taken After the Flood' by Jo Shapcott

I can't sit still these days. The ocean
Is only memory, and my memory is fluttery
As a lost dove. Now the real sea beats
Inside me, here, where I'd press fur and feathers
If I could. I'm middle-aged and plump.
Back on dry land I shouldn't think these things:
Big paws which idly turn to bat the air,
My face by his ribs and the purr which ripples
Through the boards of the afterdeck,
The roar — even at a distance — ringing in my bones,
The rough tongue, the claws, the little bites,
The crude taste of his mane. If you touched my lips
With salt water I would tell you such words,
Words to crack the sky and launch the ark again.

(Reprinted by permission of Faber and Faber)

Questions of tone

'The Sick Rose' by William Blake

O Rose, thou art sick!
The invisible worm
That flies in the night,
In the howling storm,

Hath found out thy bed
Of crimson joy;
And his dark secret love
Does thy life destroy.

Written in the eighteenth century by a pre-Romantic, radical male poet, 'The Sick Rose' can be read in several tones: threat, pity and gloating. It is also an example of sustained metaphor and use of symbolism, and lends itself to an allegorical interpretation. There is a striking contrast between its complex ideas and its simple expression. The form and the enjambement between the stanzas need comment. The ambiguity of meaning is the poem's aim and the reader's pleasure of the poem. The following are supportable interpretations, the choice of which determines tone:

- the condition of England as the red rose being destroyed by industrialisation
- referring to a particular sick woman called Rose
- problems of gardening and threat of pests
- dangers of illicit or unprotected sex
- permanent damage done by men to women
- revenge on women by men treated badly
- expulsion from Garden of Eden because of Satan in the guise of a serpent
- inevitable disillusion of love after consummation
- destructiveness of lust
- act of rape
- loss of virginity
- innocence being replaced by experience
- passivity and weakness of the female sex
- phallic potency of the male sex
- corruption seeks out and spoils the pure and perfect
- disease and cancer as human illnesses
- joy is doomed to be destroyed (rhyme link)
- appearances are false and the rose is ugly beneath
- death of a romantic relationship because of sexual unavailability of female (cf. 'To His Coy Mistress' by Andrew Marvell)
- vulnerability and ephemerality of beauty
- universality and omnipotence of evil
- life is a bed of roses — with worms in the buds

In the following dialogue from *Pride and Prejudice*, much can be inferred about the character of the two speakers from their syntax, diction and tone. However, because there is an implied presence of an author who has a narrative stance which is itself ironic, the tone of at least one of the characters must be seen through this lens. Mr Collins thinks he is in the right and is cutting a fine figure, whereas the character he is addressing, and the reader, see him as being very much in the wrong and making an idiot of himself. You must therefore be aware that there can be different levels of narrative voice in literary texts of all genres.

'You must give me leave to flatter myself, my dear cousin, that your refusal of my addresses is merely words of course. My reasons for believing it are briefly these:

It does not appear to me that my hand is unworthy your acceptance, or that the establishment I can offer would be any other than highly desirable. My situation in life, my connections with the family of de Bourgh, and my relationship to your own, are circumstances highly in my favour; and you should take it into further consideration, that in spite of your manifold attractions, it is by no means certain that another offer of marriage may ever be made you. Your portion is unhappily so small that it will in all likelihood undo the effects of your loveliness and amiable qualifications. As I must therefore conclude that you are not serious in your rejection of me, I shall choose to attribute it to your wish of increasing my love by suspense, according to the usual practice of elegant females.'

'I do assure you, sir, that I have no pretensions whatever to that kind of elegance which consists in tormenting a respectable man. I would rather be paid the compliment of being believed sincere. I thank you again and again for the honour you have done me in your proposals, but to accept them is absolutely impossible. My feelings in every respect forbid it. Can I speak plainer? Do not consider me now as an elegant female, intending to plague you, but as a rational creature, speaking the truth from her heart.'

(From *Pride and Prejudice* by Jane Austen)

Speaker A, the male proposer, uses cliché, litotes, unintentional irony, polysyllabic vocabulary, imperatives, unnecessarily complicated syntax, prolixity and name-dropping. He can therefore be deduced to be socially pretentious, pompous, patronising, pedantic, complacent, insulting, insensitive, egocentric and opinionated. Speaker B, the female rejecter of his proposal, expresses herself in short and elegant sentences, plain language, deliberate irony and categorical statements. Her character is conveyed as frank, sincere, intelligent, passionate, offended, and desperate to be understood and not stereotyped.

A famously complex ironic poem, 'My Last Duchess' by Robert Browning, makes the ironic viewpoint that of the author/reader, so that the persona gives the opposite impression from the desired one of seeking to impress, though he is also being deliberately ironic in his confession and veiled message to the count's emissary concerning the next duchess. Many students do not detect the layers of irony in this poem, nor do they realise that Swift's 'A Modest Proposal' is using irony as a satirical device until it becomes too outrageous to ignore. It is more likely, however, for the modern reader to perceive irony where it does not exist, since we are used to irony being everywhere, even in advertising. Shakespeare's Sonnet 57 says that he has nothing better to do than to wait hand and foot on his mistress all day, but given the social, historical and literary context, it is unlikely that he is being ironic (likewise in the case of the ending of *The Taming of the Shrew*, which modern directors and audiences have such difficulty in accepting as non-ironic).

The prose extract that follows cannot be read ironically (and therefore could be parodied) because its lyrical descriptive diction and rapturous tone merge the exalted perception of the artistic persona with the narrative viewpoint.

A girl stood before him in midstream, alone and still, gazing out to sea. She seemed like one whom magic had changed into the likeness of a strange and beautiful seabird. Her long slender bare legs were delicate as a crane's and pure save where an emerald trail of seaweed had fashioned itself as a sign upon the flesh. Her thighs, fuller and softhued as ivory, were bared almost to the hips, where the white fringes of her drawers were like feathering of soft white down. Her slateblue skirts were kilted boldly about her waist and dovetailed behind her. Her bosom was as a bird's, soft and slight, slight and soft as the breast of some darkplumed dove. But her long fair hair was girlish: and girlish, and touched with the wonder of mortal beauty, her face.

(From *A Portrait of the Artist as a Young* Man by James Joyce)

This purple passage is a good example of epiphany (an arrested moment of sublime revelation), sustained imagery, semantic chains (birds and divinity), metamorphosis, repeated sound ('s' and 'sh'), colour, heightened emotion, inverted word order, sensuality and repetition for rhetorical effect.

Mystification

Sometimes the obscurity of the text arises not from ambiguity or irony, but simply from deliberate vagueness or withholding of information, as in the poem below, whose apparently simple form and diction are in tension with the depths it conceals. The tone itself is, therefore, mysterious, and the reader can only speculate, based on the little evidence available, on the character and his situation, but it is not necessary to know the facts in order to enjoy the poem; in fact, it is not knowing that gives enjoyment.

'Stopping by Woods on a Snowy Evening' by Robert Frost
Whose woods these are I think I know,
His house is in the village, though;
He will not see me stopping here
To watch his woods fill up with snow.

My little horse must think it queer
To stop without a farmhouse near
Between the woods and frozen lake
The darkest evening of the year.

He gives his harness bells a shake
To ask if there is some mistake.
The only other sound's the sweep
Of easy wind and downy flake.

The woods are lovely, dark and deep,
But I have promises to keep,
And miles to go before I sleep,
And miles to go before I sleep.

> (From *The Poetry of Robert Frost* published by Jonathan Cape.
> Reprinted by permission of The Random House Group Ltd.)

The mysteries of the above poem are many for such a short text:

- Where is the speaker?
- Who is he?
- Where is he going?
- Why choose to set out on a long journey in difficult weather conditions, at the end of the day, the 'darkest evening of the year'?
- Why stop to stare at someone else's property in the middle of nowhere and when he is in a hurry?
- Why does he not want to be seen?
- Why does he only think he knows who it belongs to?
- What are the promises that must be kept?
- Why can he not stop to sleep on the journey?

Set in a similarly obscure landscape, the opening paragraph of a short story by Middleton, called 'The Interrogators', puts the reader in the position of having to ask the questions of who, what, when, where and why, but never answers them, at least not directly; the text has to be interrogated. The suppressed particular 'It' and the non-defined 'We' add to the feeling of concealment created by the suggestively metaphorical language of 'frozen' and 'buried' and 'filtering'.

> It is some time ago now. The pines are wedges of silver, on either side of the road. Fresh snow crunches under the tyres, with their thick tracks, while the road keeps turning and descending, through a country of frozen lakes, a buried country. We left the main road ten minutes ago. Now we are filtering through these layers of green, silver, and air.

However, there are also mysteries in text that are meant to be solved, and without these solutions the text remains entirely meaningless and therefore pointless.

'Metaphors' by Sylvia Plath
I'm a riddle in nine syllables
An elephant, a ponderous house,
A melon strolling on two tendrils.
Oh, red fruit, ivory, fine timbers!
This loaf's big with its yeasty rising.
Money's new minted in this fat purse.
I'm a means, a stage, a cow in calf.
I've eaten a bag of green apples,
Boarded the train there's no getting off.

(Reprinted by permission of Faber and Faber)

The poem was written by a twentieth-century American woman torn between the roles of poet and mother. The nine letters in the title, the nine syllables in each line, and the nine lines in the poem symbolise the nine months of pregnancy, which is the answer to the riddle. Each separate line is a clue, and they are linked by a semantic chain of words to do with heaviness and ungainliness. There is a contrast between the manufactured (house, timbers, loaf, money, purse, train) and the natural (elephant, melon, tendrils, fruit, ivory, yeasty, cow in calf, green apple). Both man and nature have used the female body to take over and 'build' or sow the seed of something that, once begun, is an unstoppable process with an inevitable outcome. Consider the tone, and how the attitude expressed in this poem compares to the accepted/ acceptable attitude to pregnancy by women.

Symbolism

An image sometimes stands for more than itself (e.g. an apple for temptation) and needs to be identified as a symbol. Often the titles of poems and prose works contain symbols. They derive from the Bible, fairy tales and Greek mythology, and have universal application: colours (e.g. white), animals (e.g. snakes) and flowers (e.g. roses) are the most common.

Essential elements of text

If you have got used to working with a particular approach to poetry and prose unseen criticisms, you can apply it in an exam situation so that your mind does not go blank when faced with a text not immediately obvious in meaning. A checklist of elements of text ensures that you will find enough to write about for nearly an hour, and that you have not overlooked something you should have noticed. Responding to an unseen is like doing a jigsaw puzzle without the illustration: until all the pieces are turned over and grouped in some way, it is not possible to get any idea of the picture. The following are pieces of the jigsaw that need to be assembled before you can solve the puzzle:

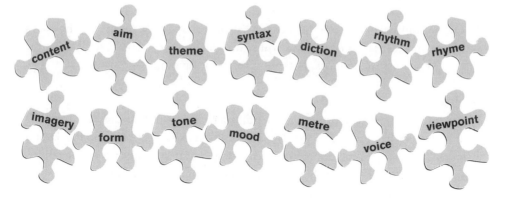

The acronym CATS DR(R)IFT MMVV is an easy mnemonic, standing for the text elements mentioned above. Of course all these overlap and are interconnected, and this does not imply the order in which you should address them. Different texts have different emphases, although it does make sense to start with the CAT (content, aim and theme) before proceeding to more detailed analysis of language. They cannot be treated in isolation and, if your overview is feasible, these elements will be interconnected and mutually supportive. It is very important not to jump to a conclusion about an interpretation on first reading; wait until you have gathered all your evidence before forming an opinion. Otherwise it will be distorted or in-complete, because you will leave out points that do not fit in with your preconceived judgement.

As you first read the text for general impression, underline anything that stands out: vocabulary that belongs in the same semantic or acoustic field; changes of tense, mood, tone or rhythm; patterns or contrasts; lexical or syntactical repetitions; features of grammar and punctuation and layout. Consider and infer ideas from the title of the poem or the work from which the prose extract is taken. What are the social/historical implications of the period when the text was written? Read the poem/passage again, identifying and making marginal comments on the details of the essential elements of text described below.

Content

At the beginning of your critical response comment on what appears to be happening, to whom, when, where and why. The content is the vehicle for the theme, and can be defined as being predominantly in a descriptive, narrative, lyrical, reflective, discursive or argumentative genre.

Aim

Why was the text written? To warn, entertain, teach, express an opinion, relieve emotion, mock, admire? The answer may be multiple, but it is usually possible to identify the primary aim from the content, genre, tone and effect on the reader.

Theme

Not to be confused with content, this is what the text is really about, i.e. the issues and ideas the text is exploring and which hold it together. They are likely to be abstract concepts, such as loss, betrayal, change or division.

Syntax

Syntax refers to sentence formations, word orders and grammatical structures. It is what happens when individual words are joined to make larger building blocks and includes observations on types of utterance — e.g. questions, imperatives, negatives, passives, parentheses — and therefore involves looking at punctuation.

Diction

Diction is the selection of vocabulary that combines to make up register and semantic field. For instance, do the words come from scientific or biblical English? Are they mostly mono- or polysyllabic, hyphenated, contemporary or archaic? Individual words can have particular associations and can contribute to the overall effect of a text, or change its tone and mood. Choice of diction also affects sound, and this is where you notice onomatopoeia, assonance, alliteration, echoes etc. Remember to explain the effect these devices are having on the text and reader response, rather than just listing technical terms.

Rhythm

Applicable to prose as well as verse, rhythm describes the pace, flow and beat of the language, its 'dance' — which affects the mood and tone of the text.

Rhyme

Check (using alphabet notation) whether a poem has a regular scheme or occasional use of rhyme, and, if so, identify the pattern and its effect on the mood of the poem. Look also for internal rhyme (repeating at the end of the line a sound already used within it). Rhyme may serve to highlight a similarity or contrast between rhymed words, and can augment a comic or serious mood or create tension between form and content.

Imagery

Imagery presents pictures to the brain; it is a way of making ideas memorable and of pointing out analogies. Metaphors are more understated and therefore more subtle than similes, and can have different effects; prose tends to use the latter, poetry the former. If we say a prose text is poetic, this may mean that it contains figurative language. Imagery can contribute to irony by yoking together the incongruous yet similar.

Form

How does the poem or passage appear on the page? How is it shaped, divided, indented? How long are the lines, paragraphs and stanzas? And what effect do all of these have structurally and visually?

Tone

Tone is the most neglected aspect of text, but it can be crucial in determining meaning, especially in detecting irony or satire, when the words alone can be misleading. Read the text in your head and think about the attitude to the subject that is adopted and conveyed by your voice: is it exuberant, wistful, bitter, resigned, whimsical, melancholic, ecstatic, dispassionate or sinister? You need quite a wide vocabulary to distinguish tone precisely.

Mood

Mood is connected to atmosphere. How do you feel after reading the text? Is there a mood change during it or at the end? How do colours, time of day, time of year, weather, location and imagery contribute to the creation of mood? Tennyson's 'Mariana' is a good example of mood created by environment.

Metre

Metre applies only to verse and was more popular before the twentieth century. The most common metre in English poetry is iambic pentameter (the metre of sonnets), which is called blank verse if unrhymed (and is what Shakespeare's plays are predominantly written in). You may also come across anapaests ($\sim\sim/$), trochees ($/\sim$) and dactyls ($/\sim\sim$) (see p. 73). Metre should not force a reader to put the stress where it would not naturally fall. There may be irregularities of metre for emphasis or variety within a generally metrically regular text. Commenting on metre is constructive only if you attempt to interpret its effect on the rhythm and mood of the poem.

Voice

How many people are there in the text? Who are we listening to: the author, the narrator or one of the characters? Are there alternate voices? How can we tell? Is the 'I' persona ignorant, naive or mad or otherwise unfit to be trusted?

Viewpoint

Where are we looking from? How is our view restricted by reader positioning? Are we getting only one point of view? How might the other person(s) involved have viewed the situation differently? (See Marvell's 'To His Coy Mistress', for instance.) Are other gender, race or class viewpoints represented? Are we being manipulated into sharing assumptions? The use of viewpoint often produces an ironic effect.

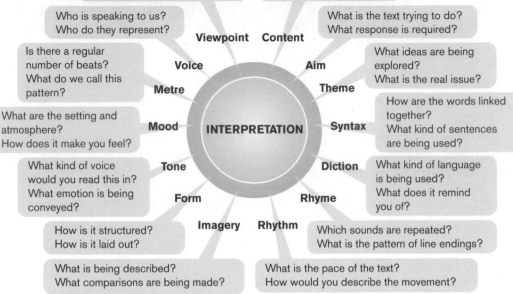

Viewpoint — Where are we looking from? Whose side are we on?

Content — What is happening? What is the text about?

Voice — Who is speaking to us? Who do they represent?

Aim — What is the text trying to do? What response is required?

Metre — Is there a regular number of beats? What do we call this pattern?

Theme — What ideas are being explored? What is the real issue?

Mood — What are the setting and atmosphere? How does it make you feel?

Syntax — How are the words linked together? What kind of sentences are being used?

Tone — What kind of voice would you read this in? What emotion is being conveyed?

Diction — What kind of language is being used? What does it remind you of?

Form — How is it structured? How is it laid out?

Rhyme — Which sounds are repeated? What is the pattern of line endings?

Imagery — What is being described? What comparisons are being made?

Rhythm — What is the pace of the text? How would you describe the movement?

Having looked at and collected evidence about the composite elements of text, check that you have not overlooked any aspect, have not missed a possible alternative reading, have not fallen into any of the traps or ignored any of the advice given below.

- Assume the presence of irony or ambiguity in some form until you have ruled it out.
- Titles exist for a reason and will normally give you a clue to the aim and genre of the poem. They can be ironic or a pun, singular or plural, with or without an article. It is usually possible to make one or more points out of an interpretation of the title or source.
- If the poem or passage contains proper names for people or places, ask yourself if they are indicative or at least mildly suggestive.
- Don't deal with the text chronologically: this will trap you into giving a running commentary, which will not focus on analysis, will have no structure and will force you to give equal weight to every aspect of the text.
- Think about sound effects; many textual features are to do with sound, such as repetition, alliteration, assonance, internal rhyme, onomatopoeia, rhythm, metre, syntax and tone. Because many texts need to be heard for the voice or emotion to be appreciated, get used to reading the text to yourself in your head.
- Get used to commenting on individual words and punctuation marks. Only with such close examination will you be able to interpret the text fully or find enough to write about.

- Students tend to write a lot about characterisation and imagery and little or nothing about all the other elements of text. Tone and form are often completely overlooked, though these can be primary indications of textual aim and ignoring them can lead to misrecognition.

- Do not fall into the intentional fallacy of trying to guess what was in the head of the writer. Get into the habit of talking about 'the poem' or 'the text' rather than 'the poet' to help you to focus on what really matters and can be supported.

- Watch out for similar or opposite word pairings created through rhyme, assonance, alliteration, juxtaposition, parallelism or antithesis (e.g. the words 'joy' and 'destroy' in Blake's 'The Sick Rose'). Binary oppositions are the basic structure underlying reading and writing, and you are quite likely to find evidence of one or more in your unseen text. Paradox, irony and oxymoron can only work as literary devices because of the idea of antithesis.

- Contrast can also be present in form, tone, syntax and rhythm. Look at the text to see where there are changes of any kind, e.g. pace, occurring within it. Is the end comparable with the beginning or has there been a progression?

- A piece of narrative verse or prose may well contain dialogue, even a small amount of which will reveal character, attitudes and relationships.

- It is possible your prose passage or poem is didactic and argumentative. Find the rhetorical features that aid persuasion, such as emotive diction, inverted syntax, hyperbole, juxtaposition, use of triple structures, questions and exclamations, inclusive subject pronouns, sarcasm and irony, repetition of keywords or use of negatives. Some language features are very subtle and easily missed, such as why 'not unhappy' (litotes) has a slightly different effect from 'happy', or how 'he has a penny or two' (meiosis) differs from 'he is well off'.

- AO5ii relates to contextual influences and is an objective for the unseen synoptic unit. What does the choice of genre, title, form, register, diction and theme suggest about the cultural and historical period in which the piece was written?

- If the prose piece is the opening to a novel, in addition to the usual analytical features, you will need to define the type of opening and comment on how successful it is in terms of gripping the reader and in striking the keynotes. Is there an element of shock, intrigue or mystery conveyed in the first sentence? Does it start *in medias res*? How does the order of information influence your assessment of its relative importance? (For example, the beginning of *The Return of the Native* makes it clear that Egdon Heath is more significant than the tiny human creatures traversing it.) Are we seeing the action and setting with a telescopic, microscopic or panoramic lens?

- If you find a text mysterious or contradictory, don't panic and present only one view; assume it is meant to be so, and analyse how this effect has been created. Do not be afraid of expressions you cannot fully explain; explore them anyway, but do not pretend to have an understanding you do not possess.

- Whatever the particular ideological critique you or your teacher might favour, do not apply it to the exclusion of other possible readings, as this can distort your response and its focus on the question.

What is the overall cumulative effect of all your observations? Combine and order your annotations as supported points into a plan. You are now ready to write a response to the unseen text that offers a coherent interpretation, an overview, a sustained argument and a detailed analysis of the close reading of the text.

Assessment focus

LITERATURE

Studying

English

Literature

Specifications and Assessment Objectives

AS/A2 specifications

The full A-level course consists of six units or modules, the last of which is synoptic, which means that it must assess the cumulative knowledge and skills you have acquired throughout the course, not just the study of a particular text or pair of texts. The units are predominantly open-book modules, which means that you can take the text, with a limited amount of annotation, into the exam with you. There are, however, at least two closed-book modules, the number depending on the exam board.

The specifications of the various awarding bodies differ considerably. Below is a chart of their principal features.

	AQA A	AQA B	Edexcel	OCR	WJEC
Unit 1	Modern novel CLOSED 15%	Novel OPEN 17.5%	Drama/poetry OPEN 20%	Shakespeare CLOSED 15%	Shakespeare CLOSED 15%
Unit 2	Shakespeare OPEN C/W option 15%	Drama/poetry CLOSED 17.5%	Prose pre-1900 CLOSED 15%	Poetry/prose OPEN 20%	Poetry/prose/ drama OPEN C/W option 15%
Unit 3	Drama/poetry OPEN 20%	Shakespeare Compulsory C/W 15%	Shakespeare OPEN C/W option 15%	Compulsory C/W 15%	Modern poetry Prose pre-1900 OPEN 20%
Unit 4	Drama pre-1770 Poetry pre-1900 CLOSED 15%	Comparative Compulsory C/W 15%	Modern prose OPEN C/W option 15%	Poetry pre-1900 Drama pre-1900 CLOSED 15%	Poetry pre-1900 OPEN 15%
Unit 5	Comparative OPEN C/W option 15%	Drama pre-1770 Poetry pre-1900 CLOSED 15%	Drama/poetry OPEN 15%	Modern prose OPEN C/W option 15%	Comparative C/W option 15%
Unit 6	Synoptic: Unseen 20%	Synoptic: Pre-release + Unseen 20%	Synoptic: Unseen Comparative CLOSED 20%	Synoptic: Comparative and unseen CLOSED 20%	Synoptic: Unseen Drama pre-1770 CLOSED 20%

The complete specifications, including lists of set texts and specimen examination papers, are available on the websites of the examination boards:

- www.aqa.org.uk
- www.edexcel.org.uk
- www.ocr.org.uk
- www.wjec.co.uk

Assessment Objectives

The Assessment Objectives for A-level English Literature are common to all boards. You should be able to:

AO1	communicate clearly the knowledge, understanding and insight appropriate to literary study, using appropriate terminology and accurate and coherent written expression
AO2i	respond with knowledge and understanding to literary texts of different types and periods
AO2ii	respond with knowledge and understanding to literary texts of different types and periods, exploring and commenting on relationships and comparisons between literary texts
AO3	show detailed understanding of the ways in which writers' choices of form, structure and language shape meanings
AO4	articulate independent opinions and judgements, informed by different interpretations of literary texts by other readers
AO5i	show understanding of the contexts in which literary texts are written and understood
AO5ii	evaluate the significance of cultural, historical and other contextual influences on literary texts and study

A summary or paraphrase of each AO is given below and is worth memorising.

AO1	clarity of written communication
AO2	informed personal response in relation to time and genre (literary context)
AO3	the creative literary process (context of writing)
AO4	critical and interpretative response (context of reading)
AO5	evaluation of influences (cultural context)

Comparing texts

Whether for coursework or exam, you will need to read both of the texts several times to be able to 'show detailed understanding of the ways in which writers' choices of form, structure and language shape meanings' (AO3), which also involves an awareness of the literary, historical or cultural context (AO5). Obviously, for a comparative task, AO2 ('exploring and commenting on relationships and comparisons between literary texts') is a key objective, but you need to find out the exact assessment weightings for your particular board. If you are revisiting in Unit 6 a text that you have already studied in an AS module — but this time with a new or more specific focus — when rereading you need to look for material relevant to the new angle and also see it in relation to the text to be compared with it. As the text has now become closed, remember you will not have access to your previous annotations. You also need to bear in mind that the two texts must be treated equally and given approximately half the analysis and essay space.

There will always be a reason why two works are considered comparable, which may be revealed in the exam syllabus topic heading, or which you may have to discover for yourself. Your comparative set texts are likely to be linked by theme, genre or period, but could be very different in structure, style or treatment of subject. When comparing two texts, you have to decide whether it makes more sense to refer to both texts point by point or to deal with them in sequence. Either way, the opening and ending will need to refer to both. Because interweaving is difficult to sustain and can become confusing, repetitive, monotonous and too lengthy — and in some cases the point will not apply to both texts anyway — examiners recommend dealing with them separately. Of course, you should make clear that each text is being analysed in relation to the other and to the topic heading or essay question, not giving the impression that two separate essays have been tacked together. A suggested structure for comparing texts is:

- Section 1: comments on both texts in terms of what they have in common and their relation to the title and to each other
- Section 2: analysis of text A in relation to the title of the essay, focusing on its similarities to text B
- Section 3: further comments on text B, in relation to the title and its differences from text A
- Section 4: drawing conclusions from the comparison, which may include an evaluation of which is more effective and memorable in dealing with the issues contained in the title

As always, focus on the keywords in the title and allow them to give you a planning framework. In order to manage two full-length texts, it is essential for you strictly to limit the issues you deal with and not try to cover too much too superficially.

Choose carefully which characters and events provide the best evidence for your comparative analysis in terms of similarity and contrast. Concentrate on how the themes or generic characteristics are similar but also discuss the differences in the way they have been conveyed or applied. Try to stay on the conceptual level or you risk descending into comparing plots and characters in a mechanical and unenlightening way. Make sure you are comparing texts throughout the essay, not just occasionally; for the higher grades the comparison must be sustained.

Coursework process

It is usually considered desirable by English departments for students to do the coursework option module in both AS and A2 courses, partly to spread the type of assessments to be fair to students who have different strengths, and partly because it is good practice and a life-skill to have time to research, develop and improve a piece of writing. It enables you to benefit from the input of the teacher and creates a sense of ownership of a course of study that a final exam cannot emulate. It is obviously crucial to be clear about the specifications, AOs and weightings for each piece of coursework for your board.

Coursework specifications

AQA A	AS	Unit 2	Optional supervised	Shakespeare	approx. 2,000 words
AQA A	A2	Unit 5	Optional supervised	Comparative	approx. 2,500 words
AQA B	AS	Unit 3	Compulsory supervised	Shakespeare	approx. 1,500–2,000 words OR 2 pieces of 750–1,000 words
AQA B	A2	Unit 4	Compulsory supervised	Comparative	approx. 2,000–3,000 words OR 2 pieces of 1,000–1,500 words
Edexcel	AS	Unit 3	Optional	Shakespeare	approx. 1,500 words OR 2 pieces of approx. 750 words
Edexcel	A2	Unit 4	Optional	Modern prose	approx. 2,000–2,500 words OR 2 pieces of approx. 1,250 words
OCR	AS	Unit 3	Compulsory	Free text	approx. 1,500–2,000 words
OCR	A2	Unit 5	Optional	Modern prose	max. 3,000 words (1 or 2 pieces)
WJEC	AS	Unit 2	Optional	Approved text	approx. 1,500–2,000 words
WJEC	A2	Unit 5	Optional	Comparison	approx. 2,000 words

The coursework writing process differs from an examination in being more leisurely and more supported by the discussion and drafting stages, but the issues of the text remain the same, as does the need for a relevant, focused response to the title. Much of the advice given on writing essays (see pp. 112–28) is equally applicable to coursework. As soon as you have been set a coursework piece and a deadline, devise a schedule with dates for the different stages in the process and stick to it! If you do not use the full time period allowed for your coursework, and leave the essay until the last minute, you will have wasted the opportunities and advantages of opting for coursework, which needs to progress through specific stages.

Coursework titles

Unlike exam essays, consisting on average of about 750 words, coursework offers scope for a wider range of analysis and a less closed response. Whereas exam essays often ask whether you agree or to what extent you believe that something is the case, and take the form of questions, coursework titles tend to be imperatives requiring explorative approaches with no imposed argument to be addressed. A typical coursework title will contain the instruction to 'Study the relationship between…' or 'Give your views on…' or 'Analyse the effect of…'. Ideally a coursework title should be agreed by negotiation, following teacher advice and suggestions about suitable titles to match your own skills, but also allowing you to pursue an angle that reflects your own interests in the text. If you are obliged to, or choose to, write two pieces (depending on the board), consideration will need to be given to how the two relate to each other and cover different aspects of the text without overlap.

Collecting material

- Reread the relevant text(s) and all the annotations, notes, handouts and worksheets already done in class or as homework on the coursework text.
- Select and collect the ideas and quotations relevant to your title which emerge from rereading.
- Decide with your teacher on additional resources that are available, manageable in terms of length and level of detail, and relevant to your topic. You cannot read everything on a given topic, and are not expected to.
- Add focused and concise notes from the additional reading to your existing notes on the text(s).
- Keep a list of books and articles consulted.

It is often beneficial to read more than one text by the author you are basing your coursework upon, so read more poems and short stories or another novel by the same writer to make you feel more knowledgeable and confident about his or her typical themes, genres and style. You will also be expected to read relevant critical essays, without being overreliant on them. According to OCR, 'Quoting and discussing the views of specific critics is...appropriate in coursework, where candidates can have ready access to critical texts and can acknowledge them properly in their references and bibliography.' However, it is your informed personal opinion that matters, and you should use critics only to support your own views or suggest an alternative, and not as a substitute for your own interpretations. Bear in mind that critics often disagree with each other and are not equally useful, so you will need guidance on the choice of which ones to read.

This is possibly where the internet can serve a useful purpose, but there are various things to beware of when you access other people's literature essays there. The quality of analysis and expression may be mediocre at best; the topic may not be strictly relevant to your title; and second-hand opinions often sound unconvincing. By all means access what is available and scan it for useful approaches and ideas, but do not use it as a substitute for your own interpretations. Select carefully only points that are absolutely relevant to your coursework title. Do not download any article wholesale, but note ideas and then rephrase them in your own words, and make sure that this input is fully integrated into your own argument. If you reproduce wholesale in your coursework or exam essay any material you have copied from the internet or a book, you are guilty of plagiarism and may be penalised: 'All work submitted for assessment must be the unaided work of the student and no external assistance may be given to the student apart from any which is acceptable under the scheme of assessment and has been identified and recorded' (Edexcel Coursework Guide). Your views are as interesting and as valid as anyone else's, if they are based on knowledge and reflection, and therefore plagiarism is unnecessary as well as dishonest.

Referencing

A bibliography is a list of books at the end of an essay that the writer has used for research or quoted from. It is helpful for readers and expected by examiners. The convention is to list them alphabetically by author and to give information in a fixed order of author, date, title of work and publisher: e.g. Bertens, H. (2001) *Literary Theory: The Basics*, Routledge. This includes internet material for which a full website address (URL) must be provided.

Within the essay itself, you need to have a consistent way of giving sources and attributing any quotations not from the coursework text. The convention is to give the name of the author and work in brackets after a reference or quotation, or to put these details in a numbered footnote at the bottom of the appropriate page (computer software makes this easy) and in the bibliography.

Planning

The key ideas that you now have on paper need to be organised and structured into an essay plan. Devise a series of subheadings that will fully cover the title and topic, and use them to organise your notes. Put the headings in a logical order to present the structure of the argument that will answer the question. At this point it would be wise to check that you have covered all the Assessment Objectives. Submit your one-page plan to your teacher for approval before committing yourself further.

Drafting

You are expected and encouraged to word-process your essay (line spacing of one and a half is recommended for aesthetic and practical purposes), which not only produces more attractive work but makes the editing process much easier for you. Drafting gives you the opportunity to assess in advance the length, coverage, quality of argument, effectiveness of structure and clarity of style, and, most importantly, to seek guidance for improvement. Read your draft through before you submit it. Have you fully explored and answered and focused on the question? Is there enough support? Are the openings and endings satisfactory? Are you convinced by your own argument? If not, make changes, as your reader will not be convinced either. Coursework has a habit of becoming unmanageably long and then requires more time spent on cutting it than on writing it, which is disheartening, so try to make your draft fall within the word limit.

Final version

Allow plenty of time for this stage, as something unforeseen is bound to happen and you do not want to be rushed. The changes needed may be to do with length, structure, content, style or accuracy. Pay close attention to teacher comments, which are there solely for the purpose of helping you to raise the standard of the essay and achieve a higher grade. Ask for an explanation if you do not understand the comments on your draft. It is pointless just to reprint your first draft unchanged.

When you think you have finished your final version, reread, edit and improve it. Correct typing errors and check your own spelling: spellcheckers cannot be trusted and cannot distinguish certain types of error (e.g. 'loose' for 'lose') or names. Is the punctuation of titles consistent? Are there repetitions to be deleted or substituted? Is everything clear to a reader who is not the writer? Is the final word count within the limit? Keep rereading and polishing until you are satisfied you could do no more. Then submit your finished piece of coursework on time. And keep a copy, just in case!

Writing literature essays

When writing a literature essay at home, in class or in an exam, do you:
- write at least three sides, and sometimes more?
- write legibly under pressure?

- plan before you write?
- check and make changes after you have finished?
- consider expression before starting each sentence?
- watch the time and stay within the limit?
- think rather than regurgitate?
- use formal rather than colloquial English?
- include a range of appropriate literary terms?
- support all your claims with quotations or examples?

If the answer to any of these questions is 'No', you will need to change some habits if you wish to get a top grade.

Literature essays are not designed to check whether you have read and remembered certain books — that is taken for granted — but to assess your literary skills, i.e. what you have understood, how it has been applied and how it has been expressed. In the following list of skills, tick those that you believe you already possess. Put an asterisk next to the ones that you will be focusing on in future.

- making connections and cross-references
- quoting relevantly and concisely
- drawing appropriate conclusions
- balancing arguments by including other viewpoints
- taking a subjective standpoint based on objective criteria
- being able to contextualise
- providing evidence to support opinion
- using material from texts accurately
- expressing yourself in a suitable register for literary writing
- communicating intelligibly your views on texts
- applying general literary knowledge specifically
- exploring confidently
- showing original insight
- conceptualising responses
- dealing with complexities and difficult parts of texts
- demonstrating reader autonomy
- arriving at an overview
- having mastery of detail
- having a secure grasp of the text
- expressing yourself accurately, clearly and confidently
- showing close reading and analysis of text
- being able to use technical terms and secondary sources
- showing awareness of historical and social background
- showing awareness of genre

Below are some guidelines for planning and writing essays. Highlight the ones you did not know or find hard to remember. Don't:

- just tell; you have to show
- summarise or narrate the plot
- assume the examiner already knows what you know
- think presentation matters more than content
- believe that there is one right answer
- try to flatter or please the examiner
- patronise authors
- gush or fall into the affective fallacy
- try to cram in every fact you know
- attempt to reproduce a previous essay
- keep repeating the question words in the answer
- ask questions
- refer to the author instead of the text
- construct overelaborate and far-fetched interpretations
- hypothesise or speculate
- labour or repeat your points
- use a quotation more than once

Writing examination essays

Essay technique is as important as literary knowledge in earning high grades. Literature essays are about argument and evidence, about persuading an audience to accept your viewpoint. A convincing argument takes the form of a connected series of points in a logical order, with evidence for each.

Analysing essay questions

Read essay questions twice; the focus is not always immediately obvious. Many of them are several lines long, with several parts or sentences, some of which may be in quotation marks. You need to be sure of what a title is getting at before you decide to reject or attempt it. Consider the assumptions behind the question. What are the grounds for agreeing and disagreeing? Can it be broken into different parts? How can the question lead legitimately into writing about the central themes of the work?

Essay questions fall into the following categories:

- close analysis of one passage or poem
- comparison of two or three sections or poems
- characters and characterisation
- setting and atmosphere
- structure and genre

- technique and style
- language and imagery
- themes and issues
- reader/audience response and interpretation

Remember, however, that themes are relevant to all essays, that responses should draw on evidence from a variety of textual elements, and that analysis, not just description or comment, is always required.

One of the skills you are being asked to demonstrate at AS and A2 is the ability to select and tailor your knowledge of the text and its background to fit the essay title. Another necessary skill is to cover the whole question — not just part of it — to be both broad and deep in your response to all levels of the question. Only half a dozen approaches are likely for any set text, though they may be phrased in a variety of ways. Preparation of the text involves extensive discussion and practice at manipulating the core themes so that there should be no surprises in the exam. An apparently new angle is probably something familiar presented in an unfamiliar way; you should not panic or reject the choice of question because you think you know nothing about it. On the other hand, examiners are looking out for and will penalise 'pre-packaged' essays — which lack focus and coherence — and those that rely too heavily on teacher notes transferred from marginal annotations.

Choosing the right question

The first skill required is the ability to choose the better, for you, of the questions set on each text. As a result of practice essays you probably know by now whether you have a divergent or convergent way of thinking, and thus whether you should probably choose a whole-text or a passage-based question. This is not to say you should always go for the same type of essay, but you may feel more confident with the type you are more comfortable with. If the question of the type you normally prefer is not one that you feel happy with for any reason, you should do the other. It is unlikely, but possible, that a question contains a word you are not sure you know the meaning of, in which case it would be unwise to choose it.

Do not be tempted to select a question because of its similarity to one you have already done. Freshness and thinking on the spot usually produce a better product than attempted recall of a previous essay, which may have received only a mediocre mark in the first place. The exam question is unlikely to have exactly the same focus and your response may seem 'off centre' as a result, as well as stale and perfunctory in expression. If you discover on rereading your exam essay that it fits better with the other title, which sometimes happens, change the question number!

Underlining keywords

When you think you have picked the right question, having considered both, underline the keywords in the title. There may be only one or as many as five or six,

and it is essential you discover how many aspects your response has to cover and fix in your mind the focus the answer must have. An essay that answers only half of the question cannot score top marks, however well that half is executed, and you need to demonstrate your responsiveness to all the implications of the question. The keywords often provide the subheadings for planning and suggest the overall approach to the essay.

The verbs below are those commonly used in essay questions. They are subtly different so it is advisable to be familiar with their exact meanings.

- account for: give reasons for
- assess: weigh up the pros and cons
- comment: find things to write about, and give your opinion
- compare: look for similarities and differences
- contrast: mention only the differences and their effect
- describe: give a detailed breakdown of
- develop: continue the argument in the same direction
- discuss: look at from all points of view and mention the implications
- evaluate: judge the value of something
- examine: investigate closely
- explain: make clear and explicit
- give an account of: follow a process chronologically
- illustrate: provide examples to support a case
- interpret: say what you understand the meaning to be
- justify: give reasons for your conclusions and deal with possible objections
- present: deliver structured information
- study: observe thoroughly
- trace: follow the development of something from its origin

Assessment Objectives

Before starting to plan your essay, remind yourself of all the relevant Assessment Objectives for the text. Your teacher will have told you which texts have which Assessment Objectives, and they are printed on the question paper. Mark schemes for specimen papers are freely available and examiners' reports give generic or specific schemes for each unit, showing how the Assessment Objectives translate into descriptors within a range of bands. Therefore, it is not necessary to speculate on what examiners are looking for, and exam practice essays should be geared towards these performance criteria.

Alternative views

Literature essay titles are open-ended in the sense that there is not an obvious right answer, and you would therefore be unwise to give a dismissive, extreme or entirely one-sided response. The question would not have been set if the answer were not debatable. An ability and a willingness to see different points of view constitute one of the Assessment Objectives and show independence of judgement as a reader. Do not be afraid to explore the issues and do not try to tie the text into one neat interpretation. If there is ambiguity, it is likely to be deliberate on the part of the author and must be discussed; literary texts are complex and often paradoxical, and it would be a misreading of them to suggest that there is only one possible interpretation. You are not expected, however, to argue equally strongly or extensively for both sides of an argument, since personal opinion is an important factor. It is advisable to deal with the alternative view at the beginning of your response, and then construct your own case as the main part of the essay. This makes it less likely that you will appear to cancel out your own line of argument.

Selecting

Depending on whether you have chosen a general or context question, the next stage of the essay-writing process may be to choose which poems, scenes or episodes on which to base your answer. Aim for a variety of texts within the constraints imposed by relevance; do not be tempted to select purely according to personal favourites, which may not be the most appropriate for the particular title.

Although the essay question may ask you to base your answer on two or three poems or extracts, this does not mean that you are not allowed to mention others that are relevant. As long as you stay focused on your main selection and on the keywords in the question, you will get credit for referring briefly to other supporting material, which could include reference to critical works, works by other authors, other works by the same author as well as links to elsewhere in the same work. Characters do not work in isolation and a full analysis requires at least passing references to half a dozen other characters for purposes of comparison and contrast. Often it is characters' reactions to and opinions of each other that lead readers to their own conclusions about whom to approve or disapprove of. Do not neglect the minor characters in novels or plays; they may not appear to say or do much, but they exist for a reason, which may be to comment revealingly on the main characters or themes. For example, Mr Woodhouse's condemnation of Frank Churchill in *Emma* as 'not quite the thing' carries a lot of weight because he is normally lacking perception. Similarly, Jimmy Jack's final and only sensible comment in *Translations*— 'You don't cross those borders casually' — is vital to an understanding of the play as a whole.

You will be tempted to try to include everything you know about a text in your one essay on it, but much of it would be irrelevant and would clutter your argument, so you must resist. This is not a test of how well you know the text, but of how well you can select and focus your knowledge on a specific aspect of it. Be ruthless in rejecting irrelevant material, after considering whether it can be made relevant by a change of emphasis or defining its link to the question. When selecting your points, check that the support is adequate and convincing; if not, substitute a better point.

Check also that your points cover the full range of text elements: character, event, theme and language. Confining yourself to a discussion of character and plot only cannot gain you a high grade.

If you choose to answer a prescribed-passage question in an open-book exam, you will turn naturally to the relevant chapter/passage. But do not simply try to transfer and incorporate all your marginal annotation and underlined quotation. Here also the skill of appropriate selection is vital; use only points that are relevant to the terms of the question. Essays are often too long and rambling because students cannot select or focus. Remember that quality matters more than quantity.

Planning

The importance of planning cannot be overemphasised, and examiners comment repeatedly in their reports of the benefits of 'up to 10 minutes to be spent reading, rereading and organising a response'. Planning is not only time well spent but the most important stage of essay writing, because it:

- shows the examiner that you have been well taught and therefore can be expected to perform well
- saves waiting for inspiration and 'downtime' during writing
- gives your essay structure and coherence, and therefore credibility and conviction
- ensures focus on the question and prevents irrelevance
- makes it likely that you will actually answer the question
- prevents repetition of points and quotations
- prevents self-contradiction of claims and inconsistency of opinion
- saves you from the pitfall of plot narration
- gives you time to change your mind if you have chosen the wrong title
- assembles the right amount of material for the length expected
- ensures coverage of the Assessment Objectives
- gives you time for reflection before committing yourself to a line of argument
- gives you direction and control of the essay
- enables you to work towards a pre-decided conclusion
- enables you to check that you have covered the four elements of text: character, event, theme and language
- means that you can decide which side of the question to argue after collecting evidence for both and discovering which has the stronger points
- leaves your mind free when writing to concentrate on accurate and clear expression
- ensures you have proof for all points and enables deletion of ones that cannot be supported with evidence
- gives you confidence and conviction that will show in your expression

The keywords that you have underlined in the title should help you to structure your essay by providing a framework for your plan, which should take the form of a half-page list of ideas as notes and abbreviations; often one word will suffice, at most a phrase, to remind you of a point you will use. Use initials for character and place names. Next to each point, in a parallel column, indicate how you will support it. You are aiming at 10–12 separate points, which will become the 10–12 paragraphs of your essay. If after five minutes you have fewer than six points, switch to the other question. Obviously you can add extra material or decide to delete some during the writing stage, but the plan provides your basic support and safety net. Your plan should be cancelled with one diagonal line when you have finished writing your essay. The examiner does not want to start reading it by mistake, but its existence will be noted and create a good impression.

Planning should be both divergent — stretching the boundaries of the topic to discover its scope — and convergent, i.e. focusing on essential elements and details. Address, define and explore all aspects of the question; you are aiming for breadth and depth, a sophisticated and wide-ranging answer that goes beyond the obvious response. Avoid using character names as the subheadings in your plan, even for what appears to be a character question. Character, events and aspects of language exist as the vehicles for the real reason why texts are written, i.e. themes, so get into the habit of planning by theme, and use the other three elements to provide support and examples. Since themes are usually linked to each other, they provide an overview of the text and the question, and give your response coherence.

Passage-based questions need planning as much as whole-text ones, and are more in danger of slipping into plot narration or paraphrase instead of analysis and interpretation. Texts should not be treated chronologically but according to the argument you construct for the coherent delivery of your 'knowledge, understanding and insight' (AO1). Giving a running commentary gives equal emphasis to everything, usually involves repetition and does not necessarily answer the question. Often the end of a passage or poem, rather than the beginning, is the most relevant starting point for an analysis.

Structuring

The first stage of planning is essentially a brainstorm. If you reproduce the ideas in the essay in this random order, it will not form a coherent whole. There is no right structure for an essay, as long as your essay has a structure and it is clear what it is. To be convincing, as in any argument, your essay must demonstrate a logical order of thought and a sense of progression towards a conclusion. Jumping between unrelated ideas is confusing for the reader and weakens the argument. If you find yourself writing 'as I said earlier' or 'as will be discussed later', you have probably not structured your essay effectively.

When you think you have finished your plan, after about seven minutes, look at the 10–12 ideas and group with brackets those that seem to belong together. Then, using numbers and arrows, decide on the order in which they will be used in the essay. Identify which point will be the basis of your conclusion — the one with the overview — and move it to the end. The first points will follow from the definition of the title's keywords, relating them to genre and social context, and will be a springboard for your line of argument. There needs to be a logical link between each of the other paragraphs/points, otherwise they are not part of a structure. Paragraph adverbial links — such as 'Furthermore', 'However' or 'On the other hand' — are vital pointers to the progression of the argument, i.e. its continuation or change of direction. Paragraphs of course are a necessary courtesy to the reader and an indicator of point/topic change. Those that are too long or too short usually reveal labouring of points and repetition of ideas, or lack of coherence, development and support respectively.

Supporting

If you cannot support a point, remove it and replace it with one you can. Unsupported assertion does not get much credit in exam essays and gives the impression of desperation or lack of familiarity with the text. The paragraph structure — about three to a page — is of a point followed by evidence and development; without proof the claim will be insubstantial and unconvincing. Support for literary observations can take three forms: reference, example or quotation, drawn from the four elements of text. Poetry and drama essays tend to include a lot of quotation, whereas a novel or closed-book essay is likely to rely more on reference and example. The ideal, however, is a mixture of kinds of evidence. Bear in mind that there is no need to support indisputable facts, e.g. that Stephen Blackpool works in Bounderby's factory in *Hard Times*.

Quoting

The text carries more authority than your own words, so if you have a choice of, for instance, describing a character in your way or the author's way, go for the latter, which also has the advantage of variety of style and of saving you having to think about the best word to use, e.g. it would be better to refer to the 'eminently practical' Mr Gradgrind than to try to paraphrase. However, there is no point in repeating as a quotation, in almost the same words, a point you have already made.

Quotation is not a substitute for thought or argument; it should support your interpretation and relate directly to the point you are about to make, are making or have just made. Choose exactly the right quotation for what you are trying to prove, and use only the words from it that you need. You can show that you have removed words from a quotation by using the symbol […] to replace the missing bit, but you must not change a quotation, not even the punctuation.

The cardinal rule is to quote accurately; if in doubt, it is safer to paraphrase than to guess wrongly. Do not be afraid of using too much quotation; up to a quarter of an essay is acceptable. However, quotation for the sake of it, without interpretation or relevance, is useless, and you should aim to use short, integrated quotations of two or three words rather than long, diffuse ones, which waste time and space. An examiners' report comments that for a grade A, 'apt quotation (not necessarily lengthy) is often woven effectively into the texture of the candidate's own prose'.

There is convention for the setting out of quotations: short ones (less than one line of printed text) can be incorporated into your own sentence, grammatically, within inverted commas. Longer quotations are introduced by a colon, inset from both margins as if a new paragraph, still within quotation marks, and in the case of poetry or verse drama, set out in lines as printed in the text. A solidus (/) is the symbol for a line demarcation if you realise too late that you have not represented line breaks. But ask yourself why you are using such a lengthy quotation, as it is rarely justified. Put quotations (and novel and play titles) in double inverted commas; short-story and poem titles are signified by single inverted commas, as are words being used in an ironic or colloquial way, such as 'fallen woman' or 'macho'. Sometimes such expressions are appropriate, but beware of using them lazily because you cannot think of a more formal expression. (Note that printed matter normally uses single inverted commas to signify quotation, since italics and bolding are available for text titles and for ironic or emphatic usage.)

If you cannot find the right quotation to prove a point, reconsider whether the point is valid or worth making, and do not use a quotation that you happen to remember if it does not belong in the course of your argument. A quotation may prove more than one point. Rather than repeating it, which weakens its effect, use it as a 'sandwich' between the two ideas it illustrates, which gives the impression of good planning and structuring. If relevant, give some indication of who says it and at what point in the text, but you do not need to give page, chapter or scene references, and never give page or line numbers instead of the quotation; examiners do not have time to find it.

Attributing

It is impressive to use critical sources, as this demonstrates reading around and beyond the text, a scholarly approach and respect for different perspectives. There is an authority that comes with being able to summon an apt external quotation, and precisely or generally attributed critical comments can make effective openings and endings for coursework and exam essays. So what should you do with the ideas you have found in your wider reading and want to make use of in your own responses?

Give credit where it is due, rather than trying to pass off someone else's idea or phrasing as your own. It rarely fools the examiner and it is much more scholarly to attribute the reference, unless it is something that has been completely absorbed into your own interpretation and is in your own words. Otherwise there is a choice of ways to acknowledge source material: either paraphrase or summarise it but mention the author, e.g. Coleridge was puzzled by Iago's apparent lack of motivation; or quote exactly in inverted commas, e.g. Coleridge commented on Iago's 'motive-hunting of a motiveless malignity'. A third option, if you have a quotation or idea you want to include but cannot remember exactly where it came from (and know it is not by anybody famous), is to say 'as has been claimed by a critic…' or 'it has been pointed out that…'.

Open and closed texts

In 2004, for GCSE English Literature the open-book exam was replaced by the clean book — an unannotated copy of the text provided by the school to candidates as they enter the examination hall. Abuses of the open book led to this clampdown, and it is possible that this change will be followed through to A-level English Literature, the only subject currently allowed open-book exams. Closed-book exam questions are orientated to the broad issues of style and structure rather than to close focus on language or particular passages, and you are not expected to quote as extensively as in an open-book exam. You are still expected, however, to support all your claims with references and examples, and of course quotation is even more impressive if used appropriately.

According to OCR, 'Having access to the text ensures that candidates do not have to rely on memorised quotations to demonstrate a close textual knowledge and understanding of particular passages. It also enables them to demonstrate the ability to select and discuss material appropriate to the questions asked.' However, open books bring their own dangers. Edexcel warns candidates against spending 'a disproportionate amount of time in referring to the texts during the examination' and against using lengthy quotation. Weaker candidates often fall into the trap of time-consuming and valueless leafing through their text looking for ideas, transferring marginal comments whether relevant or not, and copying out lengthy quotations when only a word or phrase is needed.

There are specific skills involved in making the most of an open-book exam, and the most important is to remember that it is there as a safety net and not as a primary resource, which should be your brain. The benefit in having the book with you, apart from giving you a feeling of security, is that you may need to check the exact wording or punctuation of a quotation you already know well and can find easily. Bear in mind that the students who do best at A-level do not refer to their copies of the text, at least not for a whole-text essay. Thorough preparation and good annotation remove the need to consult the text in the exam, and of course much time is saved by not doing so. For an answer on a prescribed passage, however, a well-annotated text will have margin notes and underlinings to give you ideas and support for your essay. For a selected-episode question you should already have in mind appropriate passages to illustrate various themes or techniques. Examiners are of course aware that you have the text, and its editorial introduction, and are therefore not impressed by chunks copied from either. The questions in an open-book exam are designed to try to make you think and to prevent you from regurgitating pre-packaged responses.

Openings

Openings are an early indication to the examiner of whether you are an excellent, middling or weak candidate, and it will be difficult to correct that first impression. By the end of the first paragraph you have demonstrated an ability to write relevantly, accurately, clearly, cogently — or the reverse. Students often complain that they do not know how to start an essay. Generally, the best way into a literature essay is to define the implications and complexities of the title, starting with the underlined keywords, especially if they are abstract concepts with a variety of interpretations within the context of the text or without (such as 'successful' and 'truth'). The widest and broadest application of the terms of the title to the text will produce a range of ideas that could be the structural headings for the essay.

As well as indicating the scope and framework for the answer, the opening should provide brief and relevant contextual, intertextual and intratextual information, including the position of the extract within the work and the setting of the scene (if a passage question), the genre, the structure and the themes. What it should not consist of is a full plot synopsis, a summary of the life and work of the author, a repeat of the question, a vague and unfocused comment on life in general, or a list of any kind. Only points directly relevant to the question can be credited, so get started on the analysis as soon as possible, and do not waste time saying who wrote the text and how marvellous they were.

Endings

Students also have trouble with endings, which are as important as openings. They are what the whole essay has been working towards and are what the examiner has in mind when deciding upon a final mark. An ending needs to be conclusive, and not give the impression that the student has run out of time, ink or ideas. An ineffective ending is often the result of poor planning. Just repeating a point already made or lamely ending with a summary of the essay is a weak way of finishing, and cannot earn any extra marks, whereas an impressive, conclusive ending demonstrates that the case has been proved. You need to take a step back from the close focus of the essay and make a comment that pulls together everything you have been saying and ties it into the overall significance of the text. A quotation from within or outside the text, possibly by the author, can be an effective and definitive way to conclude. You can also refer back to the title, so that there is a satisfying sense of circularity for the reader, giving the impression there is no more to be said on this subject.

Length and timing

You will know by now whether length or timing is a problem for you. Although quality matters more than quantity, fewer than three sides of A4 writing makes it unlikely that you will have been able to explore fully and give a comprehensive answer to the question. On the other hand, you usually have only one hour, minus planning and checking time, to write your essay, so you must practise under timed conditions until you are confident that you can give a full answer within the time limit. Finishing early is not desirable, since the essay is unlikely to be as good as it could have been if the time had been fully utilised. The secret of length/timing success is to have developed a concise style and a brisk pace so that a lot of material is covered in a short space of time.

Levels of response

A text can be responded to on different levels, but only the highest level can receive the top grade.

- If you give just a character sketch or account of an incident, this is the lowest level, giving evidence of no skill other than having read the text or a study guide on it. You are dealing only with the question 'What?' and in a limited context. In AO terms this shows only a 'limited grasp of literary study' and offers 'simple opinions and judgements with limited textual support'. You are describing and identifying.

- The next band level asks for wider or more detailed commenting on plot or characterisation, making connections between characters and events, and showing 'some grasp of literary study with generally appropriate terminology' and a 'limited awareness of other possible interpretations'. You are commenting and demonstrating understanding.

- For the next band up you need to link different areas of the text, enter into discussion and explore major issues, though they may be in isolation from each other. You are addressing the question 'Why?' now, and demonstrating 'proficient grasp of literary study' and 'sustained and supported opinions'. You are examining and developing.

- The second highest band requires you to perform on an analytical level, showing an ability to think conceptually, range across the whole text or delve deeply into a particular passage, inferring and drawing conclusions based on an overview approached through a grasp of the overall themes that provide the coherent framework for the text. As well as character, plot and theme analysis, you will need to discuss language, style and structural elements and link everything together. The question 'How?' is fully addressed at this level, revealing a 'perceptive grasp', 'accuracy and fluency of expression' and 'confident independent opinions and judgements, thoroughly supported, and with an assessment of other interpretations'. You are analysing and exploring.

- For the top band, you must show all the qualities of the previous level, plus 'sustained, discriminating and relevant use of terminology', with 'assured expression', 'wide-ranging textual support' and 'an evaluation of other interpretations'. You are synthesising and evaluating.

Writing

With a proper plan you can write continuously — without needing to stop and think what to say next — and with attention to legibility, accuracy, concision, appropriateness and clarity of thought and expression. It does not matter whether the examiner agrees with you; it is the quality of the argument that counts. Remember that it is actually possible to enjoy writing a literature essay, even under exam conditions! The following advice may also be helpful:

- Ask yourself always, 'What exactly am I trying to say?'
- Try to sound engaged and enthusiastic in your response; examiners are human and affected by tone as much as any reader is with any text.
- Learn and apply the mnemonic acronym ACRID (accurate, concise, relevant, interesting and detailed).
- Avoid tentative or dogmatic statements, which make you sound either vague and uncertain or pompous and arrogant.
- Don't overstate or become sensational or emotional.
- Steer clear of cliché or 'waffle'.
- Use accepted literary conventions, such as use of the present tense and only the surnames of authors.
- Write in a suitably formal, objective and impersonal style, avoiding ambiguous, repetitive and vague phrasing.
- Use appropriate technical terms to show competence and save words.
- Choose exactly the right word for what you are trying to say, and not the rough approximation that first comes to mind.
- Say something once, explore it, prove it and move on; you can only get credit for a point once.
- Make every word work for you and don't waste time on 'filler' expressions, such as 'As far as the novel is concerned…', and adverbial intensifiers, such as 'really', 'totally' and 'indeed'.
- You do not need to preface every point with 'I think that…' or 'I believe…', since the whole essay is supposed to consist of your opinions.
- Use synonyms for frequently used words or concepts and don't keep repeating the terms of the title. The whole essay is supposed to be linked to the title, so you don't need to keep saying so. It must always be clear, however, how your point relates to the question, not left to the reader to guess what the connection might be.
- Discuss the text itself rather than fall into the intentional fallacy of claiming to know the author's intentions or personal views. Examiners are not looking for an

exhaustive list of what you know about the author; they want to see your response to the text, and how you can apply your analysis to the question.

- Do not speculate, hypothesise, exaggerate or ask questions — it's your job to answer them.
- Feelings are not a substitute for thought in an academic essay; 'I feel' is usually a prelude to some unsubstantiated 'gushing'.
- Do not patronise the author by praising them for being clever or achieving something.
- Do not parrot your teacher through your marginal notes. The examiner will quickly spot if the whole class is using the same phrases and will then know it is not your own idea that is being expressed.

While writing, keep an eye on the clock and aim to finish five minutes before the end of the exam to give yourself checking time. If you find you are running short of time, telescope the argument but try to cover all your points; as an emergency measure, break into notes to show what you would have written. This is more valuable than spending your last precious five minutes finishing a particular sentence but not indicating what would have come next if you had not miscalculated the time.

Checking

Writing fast always causes slips of the mind and pen, and unfortunately these missing letters and words, misnamings of characters and genre confusions, are indistinguishable from ignorance and therefore need to be corrected before submission. You also do not want to give away the fact that you did not bother to check your work, which will give a negative impression of your standards as a literature student. Examiners can always tell when work has been left unchecked.

Allow a few minutes' checking time for each essay. Having spent several months on the study of a text, it is worth making your only exam essay on it as good as possible; checking, correcting and improving can make the difference of a grade. Do not be afraid to cross out; neat writing and perfect presentation are not skills being assessed, but 'accurate and coherent written expression' is. As long as it is done neatly with one line, not a scribble, and the replacement word is written above legibly, editing counts in your favour rather than against you. Insert an asterisk in the text and put any longer additions at the bottom of the essay, rather than try to cram them into the margin (the examiner's territory), where it will be difficult to read. If you have forgotten to change paragraphs often enough, put in markers (//) to show where a paragraph indentation should be.

When you check your essay, you are no longer the writer but the reader of the text you have created, and a stranger too. Can you follow its line of argument? Are the facts accurate? Does it hang together? Is the vocabulary explicit? Is everything supported? And most importantly — but sadly often not true — does it actually answer the question (even if the answer is that there is no answer)? You need also to watch out for spelling, grammar and punctuation errors, as well as continuing until the last second to improve the content and the expression. Do not waste time counting words.

It is useful practice to mark exam-board samples as if you were an examiner, according to the Assessment Objectives, and to read *The English Review* articles that compare the answers of different students and give examiner comments. There is no such thing as a perfect or model essay, and flawed essays can gain full marks. There is always something more that could have been said, and examiners realise that students have limitations when writing under pressure in timed conditions. You are not penalised for what you do not say in comparison to some idealised concept of an answer, but are rewarded for the knowledge and understanding you show. It is not as difficult as you may think to do well, provided that you know the text well and have sufficient essay-writing experience. Follow the process of *choose, underline, select, plan, structure, support, write* and *check,* and you can't go far wrong.

Writing an unseen criticism

Below is an eight-stage process for writing an unseen criticism under examination conditions, which should enable you to arrive confidently and competently at a full analysis of the text, neglecting nothing and interrelating everything. It does not matter whether the examiner personally agrees with your interpretation, as long as you have produced a plausible and well-supported case. The first six stages are preparatory and essential to the quality and quantity of your response.

(1) Read the rubric and underline the keywords. Read the text once to get a general idea of genre, period, content, aim and form. Answer the question 'What?'

(2) Read the text again slowly, underlining and making marginal annotations, observing details of tone and rhythm, sentence structure, imagery patterns, individual word usage (and rhyme and metre, if relevant). Look at the title and make points about it. Answer the questions 'Why?' and 'How?'

(3) Check your CATS DR(R)IFT MMVV checklist, mentally, and make sure you haven't forgotten anything. Reread the rubric to make sure you have covered any specific requirements. Form an overview of the text and decide on an overall interpretation, based on the cumulative effect of all your observations. Consider a variety of reading critiques, e.g. historical, psychoanalytical, feminist, and add relevant information relating to literary, social and language contexts. Read the text once more to ensure that your interpretation can be sustained and that all the pieces belong in the jigsaw and fit together.

(4) Write a quick plan, taking about five minutes and no more than half a page, consisting of a column of about 12 single words or short phrases. You can use

abbreviations as the examiner will note the existence of the plan but not try to read it. These phrases will form the basis of each of your paragraphs and relate to the key points of the text, e.g. 'falling', 'use of red', 'irony'. Do not use the checklist headings as your plan headings, as they will not give specific enough focus on the individual text or provide an appropriate essay structure. There is no reason to deal with the text in chronological order unless the question directs you to do so, e.g. by asking for comments on narrative development.

(5) In a parallel column give the support, either quotation or reference, you will use for each point. If you cannot find any, delete the point as it is unlikely to be valid and is not convincing without evidence.

(6) Group points logically, according to the progression of your argument, i.e. your interpretation, and structure the plan by using arrows and numbers. Put the point(s) relating to an overall conclusion or personal evaluation to the end. Start with the ones that define the genre and set the context. No point or quotation should be repeated.

(7) Write out your criticism of about four sides/12 paragraphs, using links to give coherence to the essay. Allow about 45 minutes. Appropriate literary terms should be used. Most sentences should contain one or more short, integrated quotations. There is normally no need for quotations longer than one line of printed text, but if you do use one, it should be set out as a separate paragraph. Adopt a formal style free of colloquialisms, clichés, repetition and vagueness of expression.

(8) In the remaining few minutes check through your essay, in the role of a reader not as the writer. Add afterthoughts using asterisks; clarify and replace obscure or clumsy expressions; correct any mechanical errors. Make sure that you have copied the characters' names or punctuated titles or quotations correctly. Do not be afraid to cross out neatly in order to improve content or expression; this will work in your favour as long as the script is legible. If you do finish early (and this will not normally happen if you have done a thorough analysis), use all of the remaining time to check, improve and add to your response.

Improving style

A literary essay is a piece of academic writing. Your style should express your views in a fairly formal way, using complex sentences for the complex concepts you need to explore, and generally showing a command of terminology, vocabulary and syntax. A sophisticated use of language shows subtlety of thought as well as of expression, giving the right impression of maturity. Remember the aim of a literature essay is to persuade the reader that you know what you are talking about, and you will sound much more convincing and authoritative if you can express yourself effectively. Examiners will form a view of you as a candidate after the first few lines of writing, and style will be the basis of that impression. You should be aiming at assurance and even elegance of expression, not just intelligibility and appropriateness. An attractive, varied style adds pleasure and interest to the reading process, and conveys the idea that you are sensitive to language. An examiner has several hundred scripts to mark and cannot help being impressed by and grateful for an essay that is a delight to read.

Getting the balance right

Precision and concision are also important elements of essay style; a student with economic expression can make at least twice as many points as one with a prolix style in the same time limit. You presumably know by now what your tendency as a writer is. The ideal is a balance between the abrupt and telegraphic and the leisurely and expansive. If you are too elliptical, your essays are not only too short but also too dense, with several points squashed into one sentence. This makes it hard work for the reader to distinguish and appreciate them. If this is your habit, aim to expand the definition and analysis of each concept so that it is suitably developed before you move on to the next point in a new sentence. If, on the other hand, a single point in your essay rambles on over several sentences with much redundancy and repetition of idea and vocabulary, you need to tighten up your style so that you can cover the same amount of content in fewer words (which will then give you time to add more information). As for diction, the aim is to avoid being pompous and using polysyllabic words just for the sake of it — which may well interfere with clarity and concision — or conversely being too monosyllabic, chatty or casual.

Considering the reader

What annoys examiners is inappropriately informal usage: colloquialisms, misused words, overused words, abbreviations for character or title names, numerals, contractions and acronyms. Vagueness of vocabulary or phrasing reveals a laziness of thought or expression and an incompetency in language skill that can reduce the all-important clarity of your argument. Don't call a text a 'book'; give it the precise genre description. Avoid using 'etc.'; if it is worth giving another example do so, but do not imply that there is something more to be said but that you cannot be bothered to do so. Simple sentences, sentences that all begin in the same way, the reiteration of the essay question as a kind of mantra and verbal 'tics' (such as 'like', 'very', 'really' or 'indeed') are all tedious and distracting for the reader.

Literary vocabulary

Essay style benefits from the use of a variety of verbs to introduce points and comments in order to avoid the overuse of 'say', 'tell' and 'mean', as in 'The narrator is saying that...', 'This tells us that...' and 'The last line of the poem means...'.

The following have slightly different meanings and can give precision to your interpretation and expression, as well as avoiding annoying repetition:

- convey
- demonstrate
- denote
- display
- imply
- indicate
- portray
- present
- refer
- represent
- reveal
- signify
- suggest
- symbolise

The words listed below are relevant to and in a suitable register for the discussion of literature. In many cases they are an economical way of expressing a complex idea. Look up any whose meaning you are unsure of and practise using them in your responses.

- ambiguous
- ambivalent
- analogous
- antithesis
- axiomatic
- definitive
- dichotomy
- dispassionate
- dominant
- draconian
- enigmatic
- ephemeral
- epitome
- evocative
- extraneous
- extrapolate
- extrinsic
- former
- fortuitous
- fundamental
- generic
- graphic
- idiosyncratic
- impartial
- incongruous
- interpolate
- intrinsic
- intrusive
- juxtaposition
- latter
- misanthropic
- misogynistic
- objective
- oblique
- omnipotent
- omniscient
- opaque
- paradoxical
- partial
- pedantic
- penultimate
- pertinent
- philanthropic
- precipitate
- profound
- prominent
- quintessential
- reiteration
- respectively
- subjective
- successive
- superficial
- superlative
- surreptitious
- tautologous
- tendentious
- tenuous
- transparent
- ubiquitous
- ultimate

Ways to improve

- Ask your teacher to point out any language 'tics' or habits in your next essay. People are usually unaware of them until they are pointed out.
- Join several short, simple sentences into one longer, complex one. For links between the main and subordinate clauses use the full range of connectives (about 30) — e.g. 'although', 'even if', 'owing to' — as well as present and past participles.
- Remove redundant words, i.e. those that are not strictly necessary to convey your meaning. For example, 'from the beginning of the play to the end' could be

expressed more succinctly or probably left out completely, as can adverbial intensifiers such as 'really' and 'totally'.

- Use synonyms to avoid repetition of vocabulary, but ask yourself why you want to say the same thing again anyway. Perhaps you have already made your point.
- Cut out dramatic rhetorical devices; use of exclamations and questions is not appropriate.
- Reject the first word that comes to mind and consider alternatives that would be more literary, more precise, more sophisticated.
- Become thorough in your planning; knowing in advance what you are going to say frees your mind to consider how you are going to say it while you are writing.
- Vary your sentence structure and do not always begin with the main clause; subtle changes of emphasis, as well as stylistic variety, are created by the ordering of clauses.
- Identify an overreliance on a particular verb or adjective, such as 'appear' or 'depressing'; collect synonyms.
- Avoid inexplicit and oversimplified words and phrases such as 'bit of', 'lots of'', 'good', 'bad', 'nice', 'little' and 'big'. These are too vague and colloquial for an academic context.
- Look at examples of student essays, either in magazines or exam board specimens. Try to identify and define the differences in style between high- and low-grade essays.
- Read essays by critics and notice how they use literary terminology, construct their sentences and link their paragraphs. These are the best models for literature essays.
- Get into the habit of writing an essay in one sitting. This is not only good exam practice but will give the essay continuity of thought, coherence of structure and consistency of style.
- When you check your work, give as much attention to style as to content, and see it through the eyes of the examiner.

Improving accuracy

Written inaccuracy tends to interfere with the reader's ability to follow an argument, and misspelling, faulty grammar and poor punctuation can make expression unintelligible. A first paragraph full of inaccuracies will not get you off to a good start in the estimation of the examiner, and if you are a borderline candidate it could make the difference of a grade. AO1 requires clear communication ('accurate and coherent written expression') and carries an overall weighting of between 10% and 20%. There are ways in which accuracy can be improved, even during a course that cannot afford the time to focus specifically on language skills.

Handwriting

Nowadays many students are more used to word-processing than to handwriting, and may be out of practice. The inaccurate formation of letters can cause confusion or difficulty for a reader. Research has shown a connection between poor hand-writing and poor spelling, the former being used as a mask for the latter, so improving spelling may improve handwriting. Use a pen in the exam with which you can write fast without becoming illegible, and which makes your writing look reasonably presentable; examiners' hearts sink when faced with tracts of badly formed script. You should use either blue or black ink, and there are things to be said for both fountain pens (attractive and careful writing) and biros (faster, no smudging). If your handwriting speed is a problem, it can be improved over a few weeks by practising the copying of a passage of 100 words, timing how long it takes, then doing another of the same length with ten seconds less time allowed, and so on. Of course, there is obviously a limit, and in any case very fast writers tend to be more likely to make spelling mistakes. If you can cover four sides of A4 paper in an hour, then you do not need to worry about writing speed. Reading speed and accuracy can apparently be improved by vertical finger-following down the lines — a refinement of how you probably first learned to read, by following your finger horizontally along the line.

Spelling

It is not true that if you are a poor speller there is nothing you can do about it: spelling can be made more accurate just by knowing and applying the rules that do exist:

- The 'i before e except after c' rule does work if you know how to complete the saying ('when the sound you are making is long double "ee"'). The only exception to the rule, apart from in proper names, is 'seize'.
- The double consonant/short vowel rule is almost foolproof (the difference between 'hoping' and 'hopping', for instance).
- A two-syllable verb ending in '-r' will double the 'r' in the past tense, present participle or noun form if the stress is on the second syllable of the verb, but not if it is on the first, i.e. 'trans**fer**red' but '**off**ered', 'oc**cur**red' but '**diff**ered'.
- There is a small group of two-syllable words that are spelt with an 's' in the verb form (to 'practise') and a 'c' in the noun form (the 'practice'). In the case of 'advise' and 'advice' you can hear the difference.
- An adjective ending in '-l' will become '-lly' when '-ly' is added to make it an adverb ('faithfu**lly**'), but one that didn't have an 'l' to start with won't ('sincere**ly**').
- The spelling of words with a prefix depends on how the word began before it was added, so 'dis/appearance' but 'dis/satisfaction'. However, 'alright' and 'already'

have only one 'l' — although the prefix is 'all-' — and 'full' and 'skill' also lose an 'l' when given another syllable, as in 'fulfil' and 'skilful'.

- In British English, two-syllable verbs ending in '-l' tend to double the 'l' if anything other than 's' is added, e.g. 'travelling', 'jewellery', 'marvellous' and 'rebelled'.
- Many nouns ending in '-our' lose the 'u' when being changed to adjectives by the addition of '-ous', e.g. 'vig**or**ous', 'hum**or**ous' and 'glam**or**ous'.

Sometimes apparent poor spelling is a matter of laziness (not bothering to check work through), or failure of common sense (the word is actually printed in the passage or essay question), or not making a connection with how the word is spelt in a cognate language (e.g. French '*séparer*'). Misspelling is likely to be accompanied by its near relative, misquotation, which is more serious in that it shows a lack of care and attention when dealing with text.

Unless you are dyslexic, being an accurate speller comes from the habit of looking closely at words and structures, which is a skill being assessed in the exam generally. Some letter strings are just not possible in English, such as 'qa' and 'uj', whereas others are very common, such as '-tion', '-gue' and '-ial'. Seeing words inside other words, such as 'science' in 'con**science**' takes the guesswork out of a lot of spellings that are thought to be difficult. Some anomalies cannot be explained and just have to be learnt, e.g. 'cannot' is written as one word and 'till' has one more 'l' than 'until'.

If you look back through your old essays, you will probably find the same words repeatedly misspelt, assuming that the teacher has indicated them. Unfortunately these are likely to be essential words for literature students — as you have proved by using them in so many essays — so it is worth learning how to write them accurately. Words commonly misspelt by weaker candidates are 'writer', 'sentence', 'character', 'caricature', 'rhyming couplets', 'playwright' and 'Shakespeare'.

Make a list of 12–15 words you always get wrong (making sure you copy the correct version), underline the 'hot spots' (difficult point in the word), learn them and test yourself until you trust yourself to get them right in future. The process of look, cover, write and check is thought to be the most effective way of learning spellings. Ideally you will do this every time your teacher returns a piece of written work with spelling mistakes in it. Not correcting at the time means reinforcing the error next time you write it incorrectly, making it more difficult to put right later, since the brain has put a false picture of the word in its memory bank. This is a reason for not guessing a spelling you are unsure of, but for looking it up in a dictionary.

One way of remembering tricky words is to make up a mnemonic (e.g. 'it is necessary for one coat to have two sleeves', i.e. one 'c' and two 's' in the word 'necessary'). Another is to mispronounce deliberately the word in your head so that you can hear the silent letters or separate elided syllables, e.g. 'inter-esting', 'extra-ordinary', 'govern-ment' or 'sub-tle'. The following words are both commonly misspelt and useful for literature students:

- acknowledge
- acquaintance
- acquiescence
- association
- attempt
- awkward
- beginning
- business
- completely
- conscience
- consciousness
- criticism
- cynicism
- definitely
- description
- disappearance

- ecstasy
- embarrassment
- enthusiasm
- environment
- especially
- exaggerate
- excellent
- existence
- extremely
- foreign
- hypocrisy
- immediately
- independent
- irrelevant
- jeopardy
- naivety

- necessary
- noticeable
- occasionally
- occurrence
- omniscient
- onomatopoeia
- opportunity
- parliament
- persuade
- phenomenon
- possession
- prejudice
- privilege
- psychological
- punctuation
- pursue

- receive
- reminiscent
- separate
- simile
- soliloquy
- specific
- subtle
- successfully
- surprise
- technique
- temporary
- thorough
- tragedy
- unique
- vulnerable
- weird

Vocabulary

A certain level of vocabulary is required for you to be sure of understanding the language of exam questions. If you do not know the meaning of words such as 'futile', 'ethical', 'disillusionment' or 'decadent', there is a danger of writing a misdirected or even irrelevant essay. There are some words that you may think you know because they look similar to others, but which in fact have different meanings and are not inter-changeable with them. Those listed below are the most relevant to literary studies; you should look them up in a dictionary if you have any doubt about which is which:

- childish/childlike
- classic/classical
- continuous/continual
- defused/diffused
- discreet/discrete
- effect/affect
- historic/historical
- human/humane
- infer/imply

- lie/lay
- literal/literary
- moral/morale
- principle/principal
- proceed/precede
- romantic/Romantic
- sensuous/sensual
- simple/simplistic
- uninterested/disinterested

Weaker candidates misuse or overuse certain words, such as 'negative', 'meaningful', 'depressing' and 'quote' (as noun). Certain words in colloquial use also have a more exact and specialised literary meaning. The following are the most commonly misused words in literature essays:

- brilliant: brightly shining
- comic: characteristic of comedy
- criticism: analysis
- dramatic: characteristic of drama
- fabulous: magical, characteristic of fables
- fantastic: unrealistic, characteristic of fantasy
- incredible: not believable by reader/audience
- pathetic: evoking pathos, pity in the reader/audience
- tragic: characteristic of tragedy

There is no short-cut method of improving your range of vocabulary, so that you have exactly the right word available to express yourself accurately, concisely and maturely. Regular reading of quality material over a period of time — and this of course includes your study of literary texts — will introduce you to new words. However, you need to make a conscious effort to use them in order to make them a part of your active rather than passive vocabulary. You will have to look up in a good dictionary any words that you may not be able to guess from their context and devise a system for remembering them.

Punctuation

Punctuation is not decorative; it creates and elucidates meaning. It is not to allow breathing pauses, whatever you were told at primary school. The most common punctuation inaccuracy at A-level is in the use of the apostrophe — too many or not enough; without this humble sign we would not know how many girls died in 'girls' death', or how many characters you are referring to in 'character's problems'. There are simple rules for the apostrophe: to indicate possession or omission (e.g. 'six o'clock'). The only difficulties are:

- distinguishing 'its' (belonging to it) and 'it's' (it is)
- realising that you cannot insert apostrophes into people's names just because they end in 's' (so it must be 'Manus' brother', 'Keats' poetry', 'Achilles' heel' and 'St James' Square'; an extra 's' is optional)
- remembering that irregular plurals have an apostrophe before the 's', as in 'children's', and 'people's'. The rogue greengrocers' and British Rail's apostrophe — as in 'orange's 60p' and 'leave's on the line' — may be endemic but is still incorrect, and the temptation to stick an apostrophe before any final 's' should be resisted
- deciding when the possessive with an apostrophe is clumsy or ambiguous and better expressed the other way round, e.g. the wife of the senior director instead of the senior director's wife

Commas are the next most abused punctuation mark; their actual use is to indicate a parenthesis (using one each end), after initial adverbs, to separate clauses and to separate items in a list. Commas should not be used as full stops; use a semicolon instead, as here, if there is no connective. Semicolons are generally underused, as are colons, which are for introducing an indented quotation and for replacing the abbreviation 'i.e.' as in 'She had a good reason for her absence: her death'.

Hyphens are needed to join two or more words acting as one and which would make no sense on their own, as in 'old-fashioned' or 'five-year-old'. Nowadays they are optional with prefixes, so it is acceptable to write 'cooperate' and 'redo', but numbers beyond twenty still require them. Single dashes (wider than hyphens and linking additional phrases rather than joining words together) are for apparent afterthoughts with which to end a sentence — like this one. They are to be used sparingly, if at all, since spontaneity is not an impression you want to give in literature essays, which should have been planned. In pairs they are a third alternative for the forming of a parenthesis, the others being brackets and double commas.

The use or absence of capital letters is another common area of punctuation inaccuracy, often affecting text titles referred to in essays. To avoid confusion, titles need additional punctuation, especially to differentiate the text name from that of an eponymous character (*Hamlet* or Hamlet); conventionally, we use double inverted commas for the former — since italics are not an option in handwriting — and single inverted commas are usually given to poem titles (unless the poems are book-length) and short stories. The creeping capital 'I' for any word beginning with 'i', often seen in 'irony' and 'imagination', is almost as annoying to readers as the 'i' with a circle, instead of a dot, above it.

Getting the names right

It happens easily in fast-written and unchecked work, but the inaccurate use of characters' names shows a lack of respect for and close reading of the text. If your text contains difficult or unexpected spellings of character names — such as Madeline in Keats, Mariana in Tennyson or Antony in Shakespeare — learn them. Learn difficult author names too; Shakespeare is a favourite for student mangling, followed by Tennessee Williams and Ernest Hemingway. Likewise with titles: it is easily done to leave out the article, to make it definite instead of indefinite, to make it plural instead of singular. (Is it *Winter's Tale*, *A Winter's Tale* or *The Winter's Tale*?) Once again, inaccuracy gives the impression you do not know the text very well and or appreciate shades of meaning.

Revision advice

For the examined units you will need to undertake either brief or extensive revision of the texts that you first studied some time previously. It is therefore as well to know how to go about revising and which tried and tested methods are considered the most successful for literature exams at all levels, from GCSE to degree finals.

Below is a guide on how *not* to do it. Think of reasons why not in each case. Don't:

- leave it until the last minute
- assume you remember the text well enough and don't need to revise at all
- spend hours designing a beautiful revision schedule
- revise more than one text at the same time
- think you don't need to revise because it is an open-book exam
- decide in advance what you think the questions will be and revise only for those
- try to memorise particular essay plans
- reread texts randomly and aimlessly
- revise for longer than two hours in one sitting
- miss school lessons in order to work alone at home
- try to learn by heart a whole ring-binder's worth of work
- tell yourself that character and plot revision is enough
- imagine that watching the video again is the best way to revise
- rely on a study guide instead of the text
- stay up until the early hours the night before the exam

Beware the film of the book

Tempting and enjoyable though it usually is to watch a filmed version of a book rather than reading it, you need to be aware that the two are rarely the same, and a familiarity with the former does not entitle you to claim knowledge of the latter. In notorious cases, the ending is completely different, and it is common for characters to be left out or to have their parts severely reduced. Likewise, plots and dialogues are truncated and the time schemes and settings (not to mention accents) altered. Even Shakespeare films aiming to be faithful to the play are usually missing several scenes or speeches. The film industry dictates that running time and popular appeal are more important criteria than artistic merit, and therefore it is rarely satisfying to see a film after enjoying the book, and discovering how much has been changed, often arbitrarily, or simply omitted.

It is particularly important, of course, to distinguish clearly between the text and a film of an A-level set text, and it is advisable to delay watching it until your knowledge of the text is absolutely secure. Examiners can always tell, and are not fooled, when candidates make references to the film but try to pass them off as references to the written text. It can, however, be a valuable exercise to watch the film critically and make notes on the differences, with a view to arriving at a conclusion about the reason for the changes, which will help you to reflect back on the book.

There are no short cuts to effective exam revision; the only one way to know a text extremely well, and to know your way around it in an exam, is to have done the necessary studying. If you use the following method, in six easy stages, for both open- and closed-book revision, you will not only manageably revisit and reassess all previous work on the text but be will able to distil, organise and retain your knowledge. But do not try to do it all in one go; take regular breaks every two hours for refreshment and a change of scene.

(1) Between one month and a fortnight before the exam, depending on your schedule (a simple list of stages with dates displayed in your room, not a work of art), you will need to reread the text, this time taking stock of all the underlinings and marginal annotations as well. As you read, collect onto sheets of A4 the essential ideas and quotations as you come across them. The acts of selecting key material and recording it as notes are natural ways of stimulating thought and aiding memory.

(2) Reread the highlighted areas and marginal annotations in your critical extracts and background handouts, and add anything useful from them to your list of notes and quotations. Then reread your previous essays and the teacher's comments. As you look back through essays written earlier in the course, you should have the pleasant sensation of realising that you could now write much better on the text than you could then. You will also discover that much of your huge file of notes is redundant or repeated, and that you have changed your mind about some beliefs, so that the distillation process is not too daunting. Selecting what is important is the way to crystallise your knowledge and understanding.

(3) During the run-up to the exam you need to do lots of essay plans to help you identify any gaps in your knowledge and to give you practice in planning in five to eight minutes. Use past-paper titles for planning practice, some of which can be done as full timed essays — and marked strictly according to exam criteria — which will show whether length and timing are problematic for you. If you have not seen a copy of a real exam paper before you take your first module, ask to see a past paper so that you are familiar with the layout and rubric.

(4) About one week before the exam, reduce your two or three sides of A4 notes to a double-sided postcard of very small, dense writing. Collect a group of keywords by once again selecting and condensing, and use abbreviations for quotations (first and last word), and character and place names (initials). (For the comparison unit, your postcard will need to refer to key points, themes and quotations in both texts relevant to the specific theme or genre topic.) The acts of choosing and writing out the short quotations will help you to focus on the essential issues and to recall them quickly in the exam. Make sure that your selection covers the Assessment Objectives and main themes, and includes examples of symbolism, style, comments on

character, examples of irony, point of view or other significant aspects of the text. Previous class discussion and essay writing will have indicated which quotations are useful for almost any title; pick those that can serve more than one purpose, for instance those that reveal character and theme, and are an example of language. In this way a minimum number of quotations can have maximum application.

(5) You now have in a compact, accessible form all the material for any possible essay title. There are only half a dozen themes relevant to a literary text, so if you have covered these you should not meet with any nasty surprises when you read the exam questions. You do not need to refer to your file of paperwork again, or even the text. For the few days before the exam, you can read through your handy postcard whenever and wherever you get the opportunity. Each time you read it, which will take only a few minutes, you are reminding yourself of all the information you will be able to recall in the exam to adapt to the general title or to support an analysis of particular passages.

(6) A fresh, active mind works wonders, and information needs time to settle, so do not try to cram just before the exam. Relax the night before and get a good night's sleep. Then you will be able to enter the exam room feeling the confidence of the well-prepared candidate.

Resources

LITERATURE

Studying

English

Literature

History of English Literature

Although your A-level course typically requires the study of only eight texts, it will benefit you to be able to understand their relative position chronologically and in period context, to have an overview of the development of literature through the ages and to have an idea of the influences on your authors. The features and events of the time and the character and interests of a particular monarch can be significant, as Victoria was to her poet laureate, Tennyson, and James I to the subject of Macbeth. The characteristics of a particular period, such as Romanticism, cannot be fully appreciated without an understanding of the preceding one and of what the next generation was reacting against or continuing to develop. The history of literature relates to that of music, art and architecture, so that connections can be made between the spirit of the times in different branches of culture, which is especially useful if you are following other A-level arts courses.

Trends

Generally speaking, certain movements are apparent in literary history: oral to written; communal to individual; poetry to prose; populist to elitist; predictable to original; anonymous to named. If you compare the Middle Ages to later societies in terms of religion, education and forms of entertainment, it is not difficult to understand these shifts. You need to take into account too that modern printing was not possible until after 1450 and secular texts were not available or widely circulated until much later because of cost and mass illiteracy. Novelty in literary works was a legacy of Romanticism to the nineteenth century; until that time it was not generally considered desirable or meritorious. Dr Johnson said of *Tristram Shandy* as late as 1760 that 'Nothing odd will do long' (but was proved wrong in that case). Writers were expected to show their skill by how well they could rework an old story rather than by their ability to create a new one — remember that all but two of Shakespeare's 37 plays have known sources — and the classics and the Bible were plundered for many centuries. Likewise suspense was not a commodity valued by audience and reader, whereas adherence to a recognisable genre was; the chorus at the beginning of *Romeo and Juliet* tells us that the 'star-crossed lovers' will die. The interest lay in how the promised outcome was arrived at, not what it would be.

Literature, like all movements artistic, social and political, tends to swing like a pendulum in reaction against what has gone before. Difference is needed to recover sensation and passion, to define the creations of the age, and to escape from the tedium of the familiar. It is the role of art to make things unfamiliar and therefore to raise questions, alter perceptions, and offer new forms of recognition. We do not look long at the everyday and we wonder only at the new; although apparent innovation is often a regression to the last fashion but one.

Anglo-Saxon and medieval literature

From the Anglo-Saxon or Old English period (*c*. 500–*c*. 1000) some heroic poems survive, of which the best known is *Beowulf*. The medieval period (*c*. 1000–*c*. 1500) was characterised by chivalric romances, often based on King Arthur and his knights, and Christian miracle or mystery plays. Towards the end of the period some important figures emerged, including Geoffrey Chaucer, who wrote *The Canterbury Tales*, and Thomas Malory, who wrote *Le Morte d'Arthur*. The introduction of the printing press to England by William Caxton in 1474 led to an enormous increase in the number of religious and secular books produced and, in time, to an increase in literacy. Typical subjects for the period were faith, fortune and love. Influenced by medieval ecclesiastical architecture, there arose what is known as Gothic literature, tales of horror and evil set in stone crypts, graveyards, bell-towers and castle chambers.

Elizabethan and Jacobean literature

These two related periods, spanned by Shakespeare's life and works, saw a flowering of drama of all kinds as well as of courtly love poetry. The monarchs, who were writers themselves, supported the output of drama and a growing London provided the playhouses that encouraged it and kept it in business. By Shakespeare's death in 1616 there was a taste for the use of masque and spectacle in plays and poetry, and an emphasis on bloodthirsty revenge tragedies in urban settings among his fellow playwrights, such as Ben Jonson and John Webster. During both of these literary periods — the first more subtle and lyrical, the second more overtly political and violent — wit, irony and sophistication of ideas were paramount. Charles I was executed in 1649 and the theatres were closed by the Puritans.

Restoration literature

During the middle decades of the seventeenth century, what came to be known as Metaphysical poetry was being written, most famously by John Donne, which reflected an interest in spiritual and imperial matters. Prose at this time was a vehicle for utopian fantasy, political propaganda and religious allegory. The reopening of the theatres in 1660 introduced a new and very different dramatic genre: comedy of manners, written mainly in prose. Restoration plays had highly complex plots reflecting fashionable behaviour and containing repartee about marital relationships. They were described even then as bawdy, cynical, frivolous, blasphemous and either amoral or immoral. The way of life at the court of Charles II is credited with setting the tone for contemporary drama and rakish poetry too.

Augustan literature

The new genre of novel was born in the early 1700s with Daniel Defoe's first-person prose fictions *Moll Flanders* and *Robinson Crusoe*. However, eighteenth-century poets and essayists admired and imitated their Roman counterparts under the Emperor Augustus — Virgil, Horace and Ovid — and drew political parallels with their own age. Writers of this period — which is also known as the Enlightenment — are particularly renowned for their use of virulent satire applied to current social topics and for attacking individuals in positions of power or the public eye through the new media of newspapers, journals and pamphlets. The verse tended to be lengthy, mock-heroic and highly stylised. Texts from the late seventeenth and eighteenth centuries are not proportionately represented on A-level syllabuses or much studied in schools (set-text choices tend to jump from Shakespeare to Romantic poets), perhaps because their content tends to be formal, religious, political and topical only to the period and because they are too long to be studied as complete works. By the end of the period, three-volume confessional, satirical and picaresque novels were well established, and romantic novels had proliferated to satisfy a female readership created by the invention of circulating lending libraries.

Romantic literature

This period, roughly between 1775 and 1840 and covering two generations of writers, gave a licence and a prominence to passion and imagination in literary work, particularly poetry, which shows the influence of the Middle Ages and the Gothic era in its choice of characters, events and settings. The period is characterised by a championing of independence and rebellion, by a respect for secrecy and mystery, and by what amounts to a worship of nature in all its moods. These are all in contrast to the social and artistic philosophies and creative methods of the previous period, against which the Romantics were in deliberate reaction. The five main poets associated with this period are Wordsworth, Coleridge, Byron, Keats and Shelley, although Blake is seen as a precursor, with his interest in childhood and individualism.

Victorian and Edwardian literature

Throughout Victoria's long reign and up to the First World War, when poets questioned traditional notions of the gloriousness of battle, Britain felt the burden of responsibility towards the subjected races of the British empire, and therefore duty, nationalism, trade, education and morality were recurring themes in the literature of the periods. There was an acute awareness of class and gender division and, as a corrective social cohesive, an insistence on family values, the ideal of happy domesticity and women as 'the angel in the house'. The crisis in Christianity and diminishing of religious belief, exacerbated by the publication of Darwin's *On the Origin of Species* in 1859, are evident in the spiritual angst of the poetry of the time. The serialisation in magazines of long novels, such as those by Dickens, attracted a wider reading public. Although in some ways the Victorians continued the preoccupations of the Romantics, particularly the vulnerability of children, the sustaining quality of the countryside and the importance of feelings, they did not sanction giving free rein to desire as their predecessors did.

Modernist literature

Modernism is the term applied to the influence on the arts during the first half of the twentieth century. The First World War provoked an upheaval and questioning of preconceptions in every area of life and caused a rupture with the past and its beliefs, such as in the existence of heroes. Since history had become a nightmare and the hopes for the new century had proved illusory, writers turned away from life towards art, not art as imitation but art as an autonomous activity ('Art for Art's Sake', as Oscar Wilde put it), and became interested in theory, experimentalism and breaking the rules. The new genres of science fiction and the psychological novel emerged from the preoccupations with social and personal identity. Writers tended to feel alienated from society, which accused them and their works of obscurity, pretentiousness, primitivism and immorality.

Literature took it upon itself to explore the workings of the unconscious mind as a result of the influence of contemporary Freudian psychology, which manifested itself in a fascination for sexual fantasy, mysticism and the evocation of mood, represented by the extensive use of symbols. Titles, themes and imagery allude to literary, particularly poetic, motifs and mythological or biblical archetypes, such as *The Rainbow*, 'The Waste Land' and *Ulysses*. Connotation, association and suggestive images on a journey into the consciousness or subconsciousness of the individual mind replaced traditional narrative structures of chronological succession, conventional syntax and logical climaxes. The concept of a 'stable ego' for characters and the cause-and-effect progression for plots were discarded as being false to the chaotic nature of subjective experience. The 'stream of consciousness' mode was invented to capture the flux and development within the individual thought process and to convey the complexity and instability of personality.

In its conviction that feeling should take priority over content, this period resurrected Romanticism, and a new lyricism blurred the borderline between poetry and prose. The concept of the epiphany — a deeply affecting moment of revelation — is fundamental to the writing of the period. There was a related growth in short stories and the number of female writers of them — the latter being sympathetic to the genre's themes of exclusion, exile and fragmentation. Generally, however, the masculinist discourses of wit, ambiguity and irony prevailed in this period.

Postmodernist literature

Dating from the 1960s to the present day, postmodernism shares the preoccupations of modernism but goes further in that it mocks and rejects traditional linear narrative and refuses to give the reader the comfort of closure. Whereas the modernists in their discourse connected topics through either contiguity or similarity, postmodernist writers — originally dominated by white, middle-class males, often associated with universities — embrace randomness, discontinuity and contradiction, and adopt pastiche and deliberate irony as the appropriate modes for the culture of the late twentieth century. Central to postmodernism is the author's aim of unsettling and deconstructing accepted notions about language, identity and writing itself. It tends to cross the dividing line between high and popular culture and exposes and discredits previously accepted attitudes to female, colonial, religious and political oppression. It is self-reflexive in calling attention to the way it has come into existence and to its own constructed nature. As a consequence, postmodernism makes us reflect on writing in general, and the triple relationship of author, character and reader. Questions of identity in postmodernist fiction are created by parallelism, binary oppositions, doublings, mixing fictional and historical characters, twisting well-known myths and drawing attention to the artificiality of all representation.

Based on the premise that language is ultimately an unstable and unreliable medium of communication, while ironically using language to tell us so (summed up in the conundrum of whether we can believe the Cretan in Epimenides' paradox who says 'All Cretans are liars'), postmodernism proves the impossibility of reducing a text to a single truth in order to cast doubt on the possibility of defining such concepts as history or tragedy. Borrowings from earlier texts set up echoes and also show us the blind spots of these earlier texts. Thus postmodernist writing is built on ambivalence and is fundamentally paradoxical; it asserts and then subversively undermines such abstract principles as value, order, meaning, control, certainty and morality, in the process undermining itself and any tendency to consistency or a single interpretation. According to the postmodernists, experience is just a carpet, with no pattern discernible and no exit from the labyrinths, which is represented in text by various devices:

- oscillation between irreconcilable desires and assertions
- alternative narrative lines in the same text
- permutation that subverts the continuity of texts (the extreme being cut-ups or loose-leaf arrangements)
- exposing conventions while in the process of using them
- questioning authorship
- retracting a previous discourse
- combining the apparently factual and the obviously fictional to suggest that life itself is fictive

Uncertainty of meaning is endemic, and there will always be a field of possibilities as 'I' is, in fact, a plurality of 'I's.

Chronological survey of English Literature

	Monarch	Periods	Genres	Authors
Fourteenth century	Richard II (1377–99)	Medieval; Gothic (Middle English)	Tales, fabliaux, mystery/ morality plays, heroic verse	Geoffrey Chaucer (1343–1400)
Fifteenth century			Epic prose	Sir Thomas Malory (1400–71)
Sixteenth century	Henry VIII (1509–47) Elizabeth I (1558–1603)	Renaissance Elizabethan	Tragedies, comedies, sonnets, classical verse, allegorical poetry	Edmund Spenser (1552–99) Sir Philip Sidney (1554–86) William Shakespeare (1564–1616) Christopher Marlowe (1564–93)
Seventeenth century	James I (VI) (1603–25) Charles I (1625–49) Commonwealth (1649–60) Charles II (1660–85)	Jacobean Caroline (Civil war) Restoration	Metaphysical poetry, revenge tragedies, Restoration drama, social comedies, religious essays	Ben Jonson (1572–1637) John Donne (1572–1631) John Webster (1580–1625) John Milton (1608–74) Andrew Marvell (1621–78) John Dryden (1631–1700) William Wycherley (1040–1710) William Congreve (1670–1729)
Eighteenth century	Anne, George I, II (1700–60) George III (1760–1820)	Regency Augustan (Enlightenment) Romantic I	Satire, epic political essays, lyric poetry, diaries, epistolary and picaresque novels, bawdy verse	Daniel Defoe (1660–1731) Jonathan Swift (1667–1745) Alexander Pope (1688–1744) Henry Fielding (1707–54) Dr (Samuel) Johnson (1709–84) William Blake (1757–1827) William Wordsworth (1770–1850) Walter Scott (1771–1832) Samuel Coleridge (1776–1849)
Nineteenth century	George IV (1820–37) Victoria (1837–1901)	Romantic II (Industrial Revolution) Victorian (Pre-Raphaelite)	Narrative poetry, Gothic poetry and prose, lyric poetry, Romantic novels Serial novels, political, patriotic and religious verse, social and industrial novels	Jane Austen (1775–1817) Lord Byron (1788–1824) Percy Shelley (1792–1822) John Keats (1795–1821) Mary Shelley (1797–1851) Elizabeth Gaskell (1810–65) Charlotte Brontë (1816–55) Emily Brontë (1818–48) George Eliot (1819–80) Elizabeth Browning (1806–61) Alfred, Lord Tennyson (1809–92) Charles Dickens (1812–70) Robert Browning (1812–89) Thomas Hardy (1840–1928) Oscar Wilde (1856–1900) W. B. Yeats (1865–1939)

	Monarch	Periods	Genres	Authors
Twentieth century	Edward VII (1901–10)	Edwardian	War poetry, psychological novels, symbolist novels, short stories	H.G. Wells (1866–1946) Edward Thomas (1878–1917) Siegfried Sassoon (1886–1967) Wilfred Owen (1893–1918) E. M. Forster (1879–1970)
	George V (1910–36)	Modernism	Science fiction	Virginia Woolf (1882–1941) James Joyce (1882–1941) D. H. Lawrence (1885–1930)
	George VI (1936–52)		Socialist poetry and fiction, novels, written in exile	T. S. Eliot (1888–1965) Samuel Beckett (1906 –89) W. H. Auden (1907–73)
	Elizabeth II (1952–)	Postmodernism	Postmodernist novels, political and social poetry and drama, kitchen-sink drama, absurd drama Postcolonial and feminist poetry, prose and drama	Tennessee Williams (1911–83) Philip Larkin (1922–85) Brian Friel (1929–) Ted Hughes (1930–98) Sylvia Plath (1932–63) Tom Stoppard (1937–) Margaret Atwood (1939–) Seamus Heaney (1939–) Alice Walker (1944–) Ian McEwan (1948–) Carol Ann Duffy (1955–)

Critical theory

A detailed and comprehensive knowledge of literary critical theory is not expected below undergraduate level, but it is useful for A-level students to know the basics of the different approaches to textual analysis, which they may come across in critical works and which give an insight into the variety of ways in which texts can be interpreted and the views of other readers. A multiple approach to reading text can provide a comprehensive response to set texts and unseen criticism. The summaries that follow are, inevitably, condensed simplifications and, in some cases, amalgamations, but they give the general idea of the different critical approaches, which can fundamentally be divided into intrinsic and extrinsic, according to whether they look into the text or out to the context (both approaches being required by A-level Assessment Objectives).

Liberal humanism

During the second half of the nineteenth century, Matthew Arnold (*Culture and Anarchy*, 1869) popularised the view that literature was both the shared repository of a high culture under threat from science and philistinism, and a spiritual force for national unity to replace a religion trammelled in the doubts of Darwinism. Liberal humanists took a pro-Hellenistic stance and adopted the view that literature, as interpreter of life, allows us to grow by instructing us morally and giving us the essential freedom of the individual to make choices; it is important to choose wisely and thereby become wiser. As a cultural ideal for all time, literature transcends history and the human limits of the here and now. The objections to this theory are that it must be elitist because not all social classes have equal access to literature, and that readers are seen as only the passive consumers and products of what they read, whereas the writer is a god and a genius.

New (practical) criticism

T. S. Eliot was influential in the early 1920s in disseminating the view that the author is a medium, not a personality. He wanted the text to be centre stage, not subjective, autobiographical outpouring, and believed that feeling should be represented indirectly and discreetly through 'objective correlatives'. The concept of 'wit', i.e. an intelligence at play, is the author's invisible contribution, keeping emotion in check, giving an ironic perception of things, and presenting paradoxes to challenge the reader. The link with liberal humanism is that poetry deepens our awareness of the essence of life and integrates intellect with the senses, something that Eliot believed had been lost since the Metaphysical poetry of the seventeenth century. For Eliot and his followers, the modern world was sterile and soulless, a wasteland, and they hoped that poetry could restore harmony and unity.

Eliot's philosophy, and especially the disregard for author intention, was worked by American poets and British academics during the 1930s and 1940s into the 'new criticism', the point of which was to read for interpretation leading to meaning, however complex, and a solving of the puzzle of text. I. A. Richards (1893–1979), the author of *Practical Criticism* (1924) was very influential, arguing that reading should be intuitive and therefore that all extratextual information should be withheld from the reader engaged in criticism, including even author or date. F. R. Leavis (1895–1979), also a disciple of Eliot, widened the scope of new criticism, espousing a new professionalism of critics — masculine in perspective — as high priests of the religion of culture (at war with the priests of science) who were entitled to make moral judgements on the value of texts. Leavisites encouraged a view of content as independent of form, applied their critical theory to novels instead of only poetry, and reintroduced a focus on authors and their personal authenticity. New criticism demands very close reading and an analytical attitude to language and its ambiguities, as promoted by William Empson (*Seven Types of Ambiguity*, 1930).

Formalism

A continental European tradition of literary studies, associated with Roman Jakobson (1896–1982), began quietly in the 1930s and bloomed in the 1960s. The

Russians developed a 'formal method' that was a completely new way of looking at literature, cultivating defamiliarisation as a means of rediscovering sensation. Unlike new criticism, which considered form contributory to but secondary to meaning, the Formalists gave form an autonomous status. They focused on what literary texts have in common and the general rules of literary science, noting the devices that texts employ to draw attention to themselves and which distinguish literary from ordinary language, such as deliberate repetition and ambiguity. Foreground (the unfamiliar) and background (the familiar) function together to create poetic effects; novels lend themselves less readily to this approach, since they deviate less than poetry from ordinary language usage, and are more reflective of social change.

Structuralism

Based on the writing of Swiss linguist Ferdinand de Saussure (1857–1913), this movement took hold in the 1960s under the influence of Roland Barthes (1915–80), who believed in a science of literary criticism. It rejected the historical approach to language development and exposed the naivety of the concept of literary realism. It concentrated instead on how language worked, as a system of underlying signs, codes and conventions with only an arbitrary link between a thing (the signified) and the word used to describe it (the signifier). Words, like clothes, only have meaning in their difference from other words, in relation to their context. For example, jeans are a surprising choice of attire for a trade convention only because business people normally wear suits. In the same way, a language's structure defines and determines the concepts it can express and by encoding the world of time and space it shapes the way we see it. Structuralism thus focused on the social conditions that make the meaning of literary texts possible — rather than on expression of experience — and on the idea that a literary text is composed of interrelated and interdependent elements. It was particularly interested in forming explanatory models for narrative discourse proving that all text is dependent on form and structure.

Semiotics is the name for the system of combined signs that provide the reading codes fundamental to structuralist analysis. For instance, when we read a menu, we take for granted that the starters will go first, followed by the main course and then the desserts. A menu is a text that operates according to structure (a fixed order) and to difference (the way the items are categorised and grouped). If the code were to be broken, e.g. if chocolate gateau were in the same group as prawn cocktail, the text would be meaningless and there would be some very confused diners! We learn to read a sonnet as a sonnet, and a novel as something different from a physics textbook. Meaning is to be found in the dominant cultural code, e.g. that murder is morally unacceptable, but there are other contradictory codes available as narrative possibilities and which affect our reading of texts: symbolic, scientific, psychoanalytical, linguistic etc.

Poststructuralism

This movement, developed by the French philosophers Jacques Derrida (b. 1930) and Michel Foucault (1926–84), and the later work of French literary critic Roland Barthes (1915–80), was both a continuation and a rejection of structuralism. It continued a preoccupation with language, rather than human elements, but deconstructed the codes of structuralism to prove that there is no such thing as meaning. Suspicious of claims to universal truths, poststructuralism attempted to prove that they were in fact the tools of social and political discourses which are ideological in orientation; the speaker/author must be acknowledged as having a view rather than ignored as irrelevant. However, rather than being the fount of meaning and wisdom, they are subject to the same contradictory impulses as other mortals, and interpretative resolution is perpetually deferred. Literary text is a closed system, a collection of signs signifying nothing more than other signs; it is therefore self-reflexive and non-referential in terms of meaning, or with a plurality of meanings generated simultaneously on different levels or in different codes. As Barthes put it, 'Undecidability is not a weakness, but a structural condition of narration.'

Derrida claimed that words are never stable or fixed in time; it is the structure of a traffic light that gives red its meaning, not the colour as such. Red in a different context, lipstick or roses for instance, has an entirely different connotation. If all knowledge is constructed, then it is vital to discover the provenance of the systems that dictate the dominant readings of texts. We need a perspective outside language, some defamiliarisation strategies, to determine whether language can be trusted. Rather than looking for unity in literary texts, deconstruction emphasises disruption and explores fragmentation and absence, i.e. the plurality, incoherence and arbitrariness of reality and therefore of meaning. A poststructuralist critique is therefore a creative and not an interpretative act, since it produces a new text.

New historicism

American in origin, and associated with Stephen Greenblatt and the early 1980s, this critique rejects the autonomy of the author and the literary work, and sees both as inseparable from their broader historical context. The literary text is part of a wider cultural, political, social and economic framework, which determines the moral values of authors and of characters. Far from transcending its own time and place, the text is bound to both and is inevitably political, since it is a vehicle for power and helps to consolidate its discourses at individual, group and state levels. Literature is not just a product of history, but actively produces it — like any other text, fictional or nonfictional. The presence of power is apparent in all genres, even unlikely ones such as pastoral, and they fashion the self through shaping fantasies. For the new historicists, arguments about the past, particularly the Renaissance, are relevant to contemporary situations. Their extrinsic stance directly contradicts the intrinsic Formalist approach.

Cultural materialism

The term 'cultural materialism' was coined by Raymond Williams in 1977, but the mainly British movement established itself in the mid-1980s. It shares with new historicism a focus on self in relation to discourses of power, but leans more towards the role of ideology and institutions in the construction of identity, and on the potential for dissidence. It is interested in the conservative role of cultural icons such as Shakespeare. Like the new historicists, cultural materialists admit that their own assumptions are also constructs subject to deconstruction, since all writers have internalised the ideological discourses of the time of writing. Cultural materialism pays attention to the insane, the criminal, the exploited and others outside the dominant culture, since they have scope for a dissenting and subversive perspective. It therefore incorporates the feminist and post-colonial agenda, since women and subjected races are also groups marginalised by history.

Marxist

Karl Marx (1818–83) wrote in *The Communist Manifesto* (1848) that all aspects of life are determined by the ruling political economy — capitalist in the context — and that therefore consciousness and creative thought are subservient to the material conditions under which they develop. Marxist criticism therefore addresses the politics of the world outside the text to show how literature is governed by a set of socioeconomic beliefs and assumptions that distort the presentation of social reality, e.g. the 'happy poor' and willingly exploited characters in Dickens or the invisible and silent labourers and servants in Austen. This distortion is seen as damaging because literature is a commodity that affects people's choices and behaviours, reinforcing the status quo and making readers complicit in their own ideological delusion. The Marxist critic Terry Eagleton (b. 1943) followed in the footsteps of Raymond Williams (*Culture and Society*, 1958) in claiming that in order to begin to get round the construction of assumptions, we have to ask what the text leaves out, what it does not say, and turn the text against itself.

Psychoanalytical

Austrian psychoanalyst Sigmund Freud (1856–1939) introduced into the modernist creative and critical arena the concepts of repressed libido and dream analysis — evidence of conflict between the conscious and unconscious mind — while rejecting that of the stable ego. According to Freud, socially unacceptable desires are repressed but lurk in the unconscious and emerge in dreams, slips of the tongue and in the choice of figurative language used consciously or unconsciously by artists. Psychoanalytical criticism seeks to expose and interpret these images and repressed desires, which become the symbols that construct personal and social identities. It takes for granted that the phallus is the source of authority and power.

Greek myths, particularly that of Oedipus, provided models for the family and childhood traumas — penis envy, potty training, sibling rivalry, anal and oral fixations — which Freud believed were at the root of adult and social behaviour, disturbance and decadence. These codes provided useful shorthand terms for recognisable literary stereotypes, e.g. the authoritarian father figure or the self-indulgent pleasure seeker. They also explained the otherwise horrendously inexplicable First World War as the rechannelling of aggression caused by frustrated sexual desire, a theory held dear by D. H. Lawrence for one. Psychoanalysis also provided suggestive universal images, such as water for birth, snakes and lighthouses as phallic, forests and caves as vaginal, which were adopted by modernist writers, including Forster, Joyce and Woolf. These symbols were especially useful at a time when explicit sexual reference, even heterosexual, was taboo and could cause a book to be banned or end up in court as an indecent publication, as *Lady Chatterley's Lover* did in 1960.

Feminist

In the 1960s there was an overlap of revisionist feminist, Marxist and post-colonial critiques, all of which attack the inequality of established forms of representation. Elaine Showalter (b. 1941), the influential American critic and author of *New Feminist Criticism* (1979), exposed the previously unquestioned sexual stereotyping of women characters in fiction and claimed that literature blocked the path to equality by its acceptance and promotion of patriarchy, a system of thought that has limited female expression, sexuality and acceptable social roles. Feminist readings show that even the novels with female main characters by male writers believed to be sensitive to and supportive of women, such as Hardy, Forster and Lawrence, actually denigrated them by putting them in exploitative and destructive relationships with male characters, which end with their taming, defeat or death. The feminist approach raised consciousness of what had been allowed to pass unconsciously for so long, i.e. that females are the marked and oppressed 'other' of the binary opposition that privileges males. Stories position all readers as heterosexual males doing the looking and judging; and he who controls discourse controls language and society.

Feminist criticism also revalued the work of women writers and with the help of the Virago Press (founded 1973) set up a canon of female authors rescued from obscurity. In the male-dominated world of literary production — male authors, critics, academics, editors and publishers — much female writing had gone unnoticed or out of print; Jane Austen was not the only female novelist of her time. From the perspective of feminist criticism, the whole of literature can be seen to be gendered. Within feminist criticism, however, there are race and class issues to prevent there being a single perspective that encompasses the experience of all women, and a resistance to the common critique that favours the viewpoint of white, heterosexual, middle-class females.

Queer theory

Related to feminist critique in its interrogation and exposure of assumptions about sexuality as presented in mainstream and traditional literature, the approach of queer theory focuses particularly on same-sex relationships and their expression and suppression, and thus the marginalising and pathologising of homosexuality through the ages. Forster — who instructed that his overtly homosexual novel *Maurice* was not to be published until after his death — disguised homoerotic relationships between characters in his novels with vagueness and use of symbols. Other authors, such as Auden (and possibly Shakespeare) substituted female personae or names to mislead readers, or carefully avoided using a gendered pronoun, knowing that readers would jump to false conclusions.

Post-colonialism

Post-colonial readings of literature rejected as Eurocentric the academic subject of commonwealth studies, which tacitly, at least, assumed a common ground between the dominant and dominated nations. Instead, it showed that white patriarchal criticism excluded or represented derogatorily the native or 'savage' as much as it did women and the working class. Dependent on the concept of Otherness, the critique radically questions the system of values that supported imperialism and which is still seen as the prevailing ideology in the West. It critically analyses the relationship between coloniser and colonised — with its constructions of relative superiority and inferiority — and pays particular attention to forms of coercion on the part of the former, and resistance on the part of the latter. This approach involves revisionary readings of texts covering a large period of Western history and a vast geographical area, including Shakespeare's *The Tempest*.

Literary terms and concepts

It is a requirement of AO1 that 'appropriate terminology' be used in written expression relating to texts. The use of literary terms enhances the style and clarity of essays in providing concision and precision. A familiarity with the terminology also shows an understanding of the traditions, genres and periods of literature. Many of the terms are linked to other arts subjects and help to put literary movements and philosophies in context. Knowing the names for things does more than help us to label them: it draws our attention to the concepts themselves, deepening our awareness and extending our powers of observation. However, knowing the meaning of terms and being able to identify examples of them in texts has no value if you cannot explain the effects they are creating, so beware of scattering unintegrated and uninterpreted terminology in your essays just to try to sound impressive.

Below is a comprehensive glossary of all the literary terms you are likely to need or to come across during the course. You will already know some of them from your previous literary studies and can tick those off immediately; others you will have heard of and can now verify the meaning of. As you can see, the majority of these terms are from Greek or Latin, the founding cultures of Western literature, and the rest are French or Italian, so you may be able to guess some of them if you know these languages. It will not be possible to learn all the rest in one go; either your teacher will indicate which ones are the most useful for the texts you will be studying, or you can learn a few at a time as they arise in your textual studies. Adding examples for each is the best way to remember them and feel confident about using them. The aim is for them to become a natural part of your own spoken and written vocabulary.

accent	features of pronunciation that vary according to the speaker's regional and social origin
acrostic	a poetic form that is organised by the initial letters of a keyword at the beginning of lines
advocatus diaboli	literally the devil's lawyer, this usually means arguing a case that you do not actually believe, or representing the wrong side
affective fallacy	when a reader responds personally and emotionally to a text
allegory	extended metaphor that veils a moral or political underlying meaning
alliteration	repetition of the initial letter or sound in adjacent words to create an atmospheric or onomatopoeic effect, e.g. 'down in the deep, dark dungeon'
allusion	passing reference to another literary work, without naming it
ambiguity	capacity of words to have two simultaneous meanings in the context as a device for enriching meaning
anachronism	chronological misplacing of person, event or object
anacoluthon	syntactical breakdown whereby what follows is ungrammatical
anagnorisis	moment of recognition by a character of an important truth
analogy	perception of similarity between two things
anecdote	a brief written or spoken account of an amusing incident, often used to illustrate a point
anthropomorphism	attributing human characteristics to an animal or inanimate object

antithesis	contrasting of ideas by balancing words or phrases of opposite meaning
aposiopoesis	incomplete utterance caused by emotion or confusion, signified by '…'
apostrophe	address to a divinity, object, imaginary or absent person or abstract concept, such as Freedom (not to be confused with the punctuation mark)
archaic	diction or grammar no longer in current use at the time of writing, e.g. 'morn', 'yon', 'ye'
archetype	original model used as a recurrent symbol, e.g. the brave warrior
aside	remark spoken by a character in a play that is shared with the audience but unheard by some or all of the other characters on stage
assonance	repetition of a vowel sound in words in close proximity
ballad	narrative poem in short, rhymed verses, usually telling of love and travel
bathos	sudden change of register from the sublime to the ridiculous
biography	account of an individual's life written by someone else
black comedy/humour	treating serious or painful subjects, e.g. death, as amusing
blank verse	unrhymed iambic pentameter, the staple form of Shakespeare plays
blazon	heraldic term and device in medieval and Renaissance poetry whereby a woman's body is described and celebrated in close detail
blurb	information about a book, designed to attract readers, printed on the cover
burlesque	incongruous and ludicrous dramatic imitation for comic or satirical effect
caesura	deliberate break or pause in a line of poetry, signified by punctuation
canon	approved traditional literary works to be found on academic syllabuses
caricature	exaggerated and ridiculous portrayal of a person built around a specific physical or personality trait, e.g. teeth, greed
catharsis	Aristotle claimed that tragedy causes catharsis (Greek for 'purging') in the audience because of the feelings of pity and fear that it evokes

characterisation	means by which fictional characters are personified and made distinctive
chiasmus	inverted relationship between syntactical elements of parallel phrases, e.g. 'fresh woods and pastures new' (adjective-noun, noun-adjective)
chorus	lower-rank characters in a drama who speak in unison to comment on the action of the play; individual commentator as personified abstraction, such as Time in *The Winter's Tale*
circumlocution	roundabout way of describing something for rhetorical effect
classical	Greek and Latin prose or poetry style and content, typified by a restraint of feelings and form; particularly popular in the eighteenth century
cliché	predictable and overused expression or situation
climax	moment of intensity to which a series of events has been leading
closure	sense of an ending; tying up the loose ends in a fictional work
collective unconscious	Jung, the Swiss psychoanalyst, claimed that all humans share a set of innate common archetypes that reside in the unconscious mind and inform all literary plots and use of symbols
colloquial	informal language of conversational speech
comedy	ancient Greek form of drama in which confusions and deceptions are unravelled, with amusement along the way, ending in resolution, restitution and reconciliation
commentary	chronological paraphrasing and explanation of a text
compound	word made up from two others and hyphenated, e.g. 'mild-eyed'
connotations	associations evoked by a word, e.g. 'flat' suggests dull and uninteresting
consonance	repetition of consonants in adjacent words, e.g. 'rattling stutter'
contextuality	historical, social and cultural background of a text
couplet	two consecutive lines of poetry that are paired in rhyme
criticism	evaluation of literary text or other artistic work
critique	critical review or commentary dealing with a work of art or literature; often representing a particular approach or school of literature

crux (pl. cruces)	point of disagreement between critics about words of a text
dedication	name at the front of a book as a tribute, sometimes with a short message
defamiliarisation	making readers perceive something freshly by using devices that draw attention to themselves or by deviating from ordinary language and conventions
dénouement	unfolding of the final stages of a plot, when all is revealed
deus ex machina	literally, the 'god from the machine'; a supernatural intervention that resolves a difficult situation or furthers the action
dialect	variety of a language used in a particular area, distinguished by features of grammar and/or vocabulary
dialogue	direct speech of characters engaged in conversation
diction	choice of words; vocabulary from a particular semantic field, e.g. religion
didactic	with the intention of teaching the reader and instilling moral values
dissociation of sensibility	T. S. Eliot claimed that from the late seventeenth century onwards poets were unable to write poetry that was both strictly formal and emotionally convincing: 'the language became more refined, the feeling became more crude'
doggerel	trivial verse constrained by regularity of metre and rhyme
double entendre	expression with two meanings, one of them coarse
drama	composition in verse or prose, involving conflict, which is intended to be performed through action and dialogue
dramatic irony	when the audience knows something the character speaking does not, which creates humour or tension
dramatic monologue	lengthy speech, often with accompanying actions, to one or more silent listeners
elegy	lament for the death or permanent loss of someone or something
elements	earth, air, fire, water — of which it was believed in the Middle Ages that the universe was composed, with corresponding humours to explain human temperament

elision	omission of letter(s) for metrical regularity in verse
ellipsis	omission of word(s) for economy or avoidance of repetition
empathy	identifying with a character in a literary work
end-stopped	line of poetry that ends with some form of punctuation, creating a pause
enjambement	run-on instead of end-stopped line of poetry, usually to reflect its meaning
Enlightenment	philosophical movement of the eighteenth century that emphasised rationality, scientific thought and human rights; it led to the rise of democracy and contributed to the French and American Revolutions
epic	long narrative poem telling a tale of heroic achievements over a period of time, often related to national identity and with supernatural elements
epigram	short, concise, original and witty saying, often including rhyme, alliteration, assonance or antithesis
epigraph	inscription at the head of a chapter/book
epiphany	sudden and striking revelation of the essence of something sublime
epistolary	taking the form of letters or exchange of letters
epitaph	words engraved upon a tombstone
epithet	recurring characteristic adjective affixed to a name, especially in epic, e.g. 'wily Odysseus'
eponymous	main character after whom a work is named, e.g. *Jane Eyre*
eternal verities	fundamental and permanent truths of human existence
eulogy	speech or writing in praise of someone or something
euphemism	tactful word or phrase to refer to something unpleasant or offensive
euphonious	pleasant sounding, as opposed to cacophonous
fable	short fictitious tale conveying a moral, often involving animals or legendary figures
fabliau (pl. fabliaux)	short medieval tale in rhyme, of a coarsely comic and satirical nature
fantasy	genre of fiction fully or partially set in an imaginary world less technologically developed than the present (e.g. *Lord of the Rings*)
farce	improbable and absurd dramatic events to excite laughter
figurative	using imagery; non-literal use of language

flat and round characters	definition of characters in novels coined by E. M. Forster to distinguish those capable of surprising the reader (round) from those entirely consistent and predictable (flat); another way of distinguishing between fully developed characterisation and caricature
foot/feet	division of syllables into a repeated metrical unit in a line of poetry
form	the way a text is divided and organised, the shape of a text on the page
framing	a story within which another story is presented, for parallel or contrast
free indirect speech	use in narrative of a character's spoken words, without attribution or inverted commas
free verse	poetry without a regular metrical pattern or rhyme
Freudian	reference to the belief of the Austrian psychoanalyst that early childhood experience affects all adult responses to life through the workings of the subconscious, where repressed urges lurk and reveal themselves in dreams and through 'Freudian slips'
genre	type or form of writing with identifiable characteristics, e.g. fairy tale
Gothic	medieval genre, revived in the late eighteenth century, which contains violence, death, horror, the supernatural and the macabre; set in eerie ancient buildings, such as castles, during darkness and bad weather
half-rhyme	words that almost rhyme, e.g. polish/relish
heroic couplets	iambic pentameter rhymed in pairs; used in epic and mock heroic poetry
hubris and Nemesis	overreaching of a human who aspires to divine power or status, resulting in downfall, which is the punishment by Nemesis, goddess of retribution
humours	four bodily fluids produced by different organs (and related to one of the elements), an excess of which caused particular temperaments: yellow bile (anger), blood (happiness), phlegm (calm) and black bile (melancholy)
hyperbole	deliberate exaggeration for effect, e.g. 'I've been waiting for aeons'
iambic pentameter	five feet of iambs, i.e. unstressed/stressed alternating syllables; tetrameter has four feet and hexameter (alexandrines) has six

idiolect	style of speech peculiar to an individual character and recognisable as such
imagery	descriptive language appealing to the senses; imagery may be sustained or recurring throughout texts, usually in the form of simile or metaphor
in medias res	beginning a text in the middle of an event or conversation
intentional fallacy	unprovable and irrelevant assumptions made by the reader about authorial intention
internal rhyme	placement of rhyming words within a line of poetry
intertextuality	relationship between one text and another
intrusive narrator	narrator who addresses the reader or interpolates comments
invocation	summoning a divinity or muse to aid the speaker/writer
irony	language intended to mean the opposite of the words expressed; or amusing or cruel reversal of an outcome expected, intended or deserved; situation in which one is mocked by fate or the facts
juxtaposition	placing side by side for (ironic) contrast of interpretation
kitchen-sink drama	set in a typical household and reflecting the activities and conversations of routine domestic life, this genre of modern drama, popular in the 1960s, purports to portray reality
legend	story about historical figures that exaggerates their qualities or feats
litotes	expressing an affirmative by the negative of its contrary, e.g. 'not bad' for 'good'
love triangle	three-way romantic situation involving two men and one woman or vice versa; the plot basis for many comedies and tragedies
lyrical	expression of strong feelings, usually love; suggestive of music
Machiavellian	early sixteenth-century political philosophy, proposed by the Italian Niccolò Machiavelli in the book *The Prince*, which recommended ruthless self-interest and unethical methods to gain political power
magical realism	twentieth-century description of a work that interweaves realistic details with supernatural and dream-like mythical elements in an everyday setting

malapropism	ludicrous misuse of a word in mistake for one resembling it
masque	courtly spectacle involving masked performers dancing and acting
meiosis	understatement, the opposite of hyperbole, e.g. 'he has a penny or two'
melodrama	sensational play with stereotyped characters, popular in the nineteenth century
Mephistopheles	sneering, clever tempter and agent of the devil in the late medieval Faust legend, who bargained for and won human souls
metaphor	suppressed comparison implied not stated, e.g. 'the wind roared'
metaphysical	philosophical concern with abstract reasoning; far-fetched imagery and fanciful comparisons associated with a school of seventeenth-century poets
metonymy	substituting an attribute for the thing itself, e.g. 'crown' for monarchy
metre	regular series of stressed and unstressed syllables in a line of poetry; the most common metre in English verse is iambic, which exists in pentameter, tetrameter and hexameter
micro/macrocosm	occurrences and states in the individual, e.g. conflict, which are magnified and reflected in larger contexts, e.g. civil war
mock heroic	using epic/heroic style for trivial events in order to ridicule both
monologue	extended speech or thought process by one character
myth	fiction involving supernatural beings that explains natural and social phenomena and embodies traditional and popular ideas
naive narrator	child or imperceptive persona who tells a story without understanding its significance; device for creating irony, e.g. Leo in *The Go-Between*
narrative	connected and usually chronological series of events to form a story
negative capability	desired state for a poet: 'capable of being in uncertainties, mysteries, doubts, without any irritable reaching after fact and reason' (Keats)
neologism	creation of a new word, usually in poetry
objective correlative	T. S. Eliot stipulated that there should be an equality

	of intensity between the feelings aroused and the cause of the arousal; he claimed that Hamlet's state of emotion was excessive in relation to the facts
ode	lengthy lyrical and reflective poem addressed to the subject
onomatopoeia	words that imitate the sound being described, e.g. 'sizzling', 'miaow'
organic creation	belief espoused by Romantic poets that artistic creation should arrive fully formed from the unconscious mind, like a plant from a seed, and not be tinkered with or given added artifice, such as rhyme
oxymoron	two contradictory terms united in a single phrase, e.g. 'bitter sweet'
paradox	self-contradictory truth
parody	imitation and exaggeration of style for the purpose of humour and ridicule
pastiche	literary composition made up of fragments of different styles
pastoral	simple, innocent and idyllic rural existence among shepherds, deriving from the golden age of Arcadia in ancient Greece
pathetic fallacy	attributing emotions to inanimate objects, usually elements of nature, to represent the persona's feelings, e.g. describing the sky as melancholy
pathos	evocation of pity by a situation of suffering and helplessness
peripeteia	sudden reversal of fortune for a literary character
periphrasis	expressing something in an unnecessarily lengthy and indirect way
persona	created voice within a text who plays the role of narrator/speaker
personification	human embodiment of an abstraction or object, using a capital letter or he or she
philistinism	attitude of ignorance and contempt for artistic works and cultural values
picaresque	narrative dealing with criminal and low-life characters
plot	cause-and-effect sequence of events resulting from characters' actions
plurality	possible multiple meanings of a text
poetic justice	appropriate and often ironic rewarding of virtue and punishment of evil

poetic licence	liberties taken by writers with the rules of grammar and vocabulary
poet laureate	established national poet appointed to the royal court, who is required to write poems for state occasions in return for an annual stipend
portmanteau	joining two existing words to form one new one, e.g. 'brunch', 'soothier'
pre-Raphaelite	artistic movement of the mid-nineteenth century that sought to infuse art with moral qualities through the depiction of nature and worthy themes; it considered art from Raphael (1483–1520) onwards to be morally degenerate
prolix	tediously wordy
protagonist	principal character in a drama or literary work
pun	use of a word with a double meaning for humorous or ironic effect
puritanism	extreme Protestant belief, powerful under Cromwell in the mid-seventeenth century, that physical pleasure or enjoyment of art is spiritually dangerous
purple passage	prose passage of ornate language and heightened emotion
quatrain	four-lined stanza or group of four lines distinguished by a rhyme scheme
Rabelais	early sixteenth-century French writer of ribaldry obsessed with sexual acts and bodily functions
realism and idealism	associated with the rise of the novel in the early eighteenth century, realism refers to the depiction of detailed, accurately observed scenery, objects, characters and behaviours; it contrasts with idealism, which filters out unpalatable realities and individual experience or perception
reflective	revealing the thoughts of a writer or character
refrain	repetition of line(s) at end of a verse or between verses, especially in a ballad
register	type of expression, level of formality
reification	describing a person or abstract concept as an object (common in Dickens)
Renaissance	originating in Italy, the revival of the arts under the influence of classical models in the fifteenth and sixteenth centuries in western Europe
rhetoric	art of persuasion using emotive language and stylistic

	devices, e.g. triple structures, rhetorical questions
rhyme	repetition of a vowel sound in words at the end of lines of poetry (masculine rhyme accents the final syllable; feminine rhyme the penultimate syllable); half-rhyme changes the vowel but not the consonants, e.g. 'mystery' and 'mastery'; couplets rhyme consecutively (*aabb*); alternates rhyme alternately (*abab*)
rhythm	pace and sound pattern of writing, created by metre, vowel length, syntax and punctuation
romance	story of love and heroism, deriving from medieval court life and fairy tale
Romanticism	influential artistic movement of the late eighteenth and early nineteenth centuries, characterised by the rebellious assertion of the individual and a belief in the spiritual correspondence between man and nature
satire	exposing of vice or foolishness of a person or institution to ridicule
scansion	system of notation for marking stressed (/) and unstressed (~) syllables in a line of metrical verse
science fiction	genre of fiction either set in the future or in which a more technologically developed society interacts with the present
semantic field	group of words with a thematic relationship, e.g. cross, candle, gold
semantics	study of the influence of words on thought and behaviour
semiotics	theory of signs used as codes in a text
seven deadly sins	the medieval Catholic Church preached that these sins were mortal and led straight to hell: pride, envy, gluttony, lechery, avarice, wrath and sloth
simile	comparison introduced by 'as' or 'like'; epic simile is a lengthy and detailed analogy
soliloquy	speech by a character alone on stage that reveals his or her thoughts
sonnet	lyrical poem of 14 lines of rhymed iambic pentameter, either an octet and sestet (Petrarchan) or three quatrains and a couplet (Shakespearean)
stanza	another term for a verse; there are various forms depending on the number of lines and type of rhyme scheme

stereotype	a category of person with typical characteristics, often used for mockery
stream of consciousness	method used by modern novelists to relate the inmost thoughts and feelings of characters without logical sequence, syntax or (sometimes) punctuation, on the grounds that in reality thought processes are free from such restraints; notably used by James Joyce in *Ulysses*
style	selection and organisation of language elements, related to genre or individual user of language
surrealism	literary and artistic movement that began in Paris about 1924, typified by the juxtaposition of incongruous ideas or objects in an attempt to express the subconscious freed from the controls of reason and narrative sequence, as in dreams. It influenced the stream of consciousness technique in novels during the same modernist period
swan song	legend that mute swans sing once only, with haunting pathos, immediately prior to their death; hence, used of any final work or dying speech
symbol	object, person or event that represents something more than itself
synecdoche	substitution of the part for the whole or vice versa, e.g. 'factory hands'
synopsis	summary of plot
syntax	arrangement of grammar and word order in sentence construction
tautology	extra word in a phrase that unnecessarily repeats an idea
theme	abstract idea or issue explored in a text
tone	emotional aspect of the voice of a text, e.g. 'bitter', 'exuberant'
tragedy	play or literary work of a predominantly sorrowful nature, traditionally concerning kings or rulers, having a disastrous and fatal conclusion; characterised by waste, loss and a fall from power
trope	affected figure of speech for decorative effect
unities	three principles of dramatic composition, deriving from Aristotle, whereby a play should consist of one related series of actions, occur within one day and happen in one place. Shakespeare pays respect to them in *The Tempest* and some modern playwrights have

	faithfully observed them, such as Tennessee Williams in *Cat on a Hot Tin Roof*
utopia and dystopia	fantasy of an ideal form of government and society, inspired by Plato's *Republic*; in literature, attempts to create utopias result in their opposite, i.e. repressive totalitarian dystopias, e.g. in *The Handmaid's Tale*
willing suspension of disbelief	Coleridge's expression to describe how an audience does not expect rules of realism to apply to drama and will accept theatrical conventions as an act of 'poetic faith'
wit	intelligent verbal humour
zeugma	yoking together of two incongruous nouns through their shared grammatical structure, e.g. 'he left in a bad mood and a taxi'

Further reading

Many of the works below are on English undergraduate reading lists and bibliographies, but they are also relevant to A-level, depending on the genres, periods and texts chosen from the specification.

Abrams, M. H. (1972) *The Mirror and the Lamp*, Oxford University Press.

Adair, G. (1986) *Myths and Memories*, Fontana.

Adair, G. (1993) *The Death of the Author*, Minerva.

Allen, G. (2000) *Intertextuality*, Routledge.

Barthes, R. (1993) *Mythologies*, Vintage.

Berger, J. (1977) *Ways of Seeing*, Penguin.

Bertens, H. (2001) *Literary Theory: The Basics*, Routledge.

Booth, W. (1983) *The Rhetoric of Fiction*, University of Chicago Press.

Butler, J. (1990) *Gender Trouble: Feminism and the Subversion of Beauty*, Routledge.

Cameron, D. (1990) *The Feminist Critique of Language*, Routledge.

Carey, J. (1992) *The Intellectuals and the Masses*, Faber.

Carter, R. and McRae, J. (2001) *The Routledge History of Literature in English*, Routledge.

Carter, R. and McRae, J. (eds) (2001) *Language, Literature and the Learner: Creative Classroom Practice*, Longman.

Croft, S. and Cross, H. (2001) *Literature, Criticism and Style*, Oxford University Press.

Culler, J. (1997) *Literary Theory: A Very Short Introduction*, Oxford University Press.

Eaglestone, R. (2000) *Doing English*, Routledge.

Eagleton, T. (1983) *Literary Theory: An Introduction*, Blackwell.

Empson, W. (1973) *Seven Types of Ambiguity*, Penguin.

Forster, E. M. (1967) *Aspects of the Novel*, Penguin.

Gilbert, S. and Gubar, S. (1979) *The Madwoman in the Attic*, Yale.

Keith, G. (1999) *Language and Literature*, Hodder & Stoughton.

Kermode, F. (2001) *Shakespeare's Language*, Penguin.

Lawrence, D. H. (1985) *Study of Thomas Hardy*, Cambridge University Press.

Lodge, D. (1981) *Working with Structuralism: Essays and Reviews on Nineteenth- and Twentieth-Century Literature*, Routledge.

Lodge, D. (1993) *The Art of Fiction*, Penguin.

Lodge, D. (ed.) (1998) *Modern Criticism and Theory: A Reader*, Longman.

Moon, B. (1999) *Literary Terms: A Practical Glossary*, English and Media Centre.

Morgan, W. (1997) *Critical Literacy in the Classroom*, Routledge.

Myszor, F. (2001) *The Modern Short Story*, Cambridge University Press.

Richards, I. A. (1964) *Practical Criticism*, Routledge.

Russell, S. (1993) *Grammar, Structure and Style*, Oxford University Press.

Scott, P. (1989) *Reconstructing A-level English*, Open University Press.

Showalter, E. (1999) *A Literature of Their Own*, Virago.

Spurgeon, C. (1989) *Shakespeare's Imagery and What It Tells Us*, Cambridge University Press.

Taylor, G. (1989) *Reinventing Shakespeare*, Hogarth Press.

Weldon, F. (1984) *Letters to Alice*, Michael Joseph.

Williams, R. (1990) *Culture and Society 1780–1950*, Hogarth Press.

An excellent guide to resources for the study of English Literature on the internet, including electronic versions of texts, is to be found at:

www.english-literature.org/resources/